CW00971455

Junior
MASTERCHEF
1995

Junior MASTERCHEF 1995

FOREWORD BY LOYD GROSSMAN

VERMILION
LONDON

First published 1995

13 5 7 9 10 8 6 4 2

Compilation copyright © Union Pictures 1995
Recipes © The Contributors 1995
Foreword © Loyd Grossman 1995
Introduction © Richard Bryan 1995
Illustrations © Random House UK Ltd 1995
Front cover photograph © Random House UK Ltd 1995
Back cover photograph © Richard Farley 1995

All rights reserved. No part of this publication may be reproduced, stored in a retrieval system, or
transmitted in any form or by any means, electronic, mechanical, photocopying, recording or
otherwise, without prior permission of the copyright owners.

First published in the United Kingdom in 1995 by Vermilion
an imprint of Ebury Press, Random House, 20 Vauxhall Bridge Road, London SW1V 2SA

Random House Australia (Pty) Limited
20 Alfred Street, Milsons Point, Sydney,
New South Wales 2061, Australia

Random House New Zealand Limited
18 Poland Road, Glenfield
Auckland 10, New Zealand

Random House South Africa (Pty) Limited
PO BOX 337, Bergvlei, South Africa

Random House UK Limited Reg. No. 954009

A CIP catalogue record for this book is available from the British Library

ISBN: 0 09 180668 2

Junior MasterChef 1995
A Union Pictures production for BBC North

Series devised by Franc Roddam
Executive Producers: Bradley Adams and Richard Kalms
Producer and Director: Richard Bryan
Associate Producer: Glynis Robertson
Production Co-ordinators: Julie Dixon and Julia Park
Researchers: Melanie Jappy and Claire Davies

General Editor: Janet Illsley
Recipe Editor: Maureen Callis
Design: Clive Dorman
Illustrations: Madeleine David

Typeset by Clive Dorman & Co., Ham, Surrey
Printed and bound in Spain by Graficas Estella

Papers used by Ebury Press are natural, recyclable products made from wood grown
in sustainable forests.

Contents

Foreword

Viewers, contestants and their families usually get around to asking me the question: "Er, by the way, can you actually cook?" The answer is "Yes" I can actually cook, although I would hate to make any claims about how good my cooking is. Perhaps more to the point is the fact that looking around the Junior MasterChef production office it seems that everyone else can cook – and a lot of them a darned sight better than I can!

Richard Bryan, our producer/director, is an inspired Aga lout more often found happily ensconced in his Norfolk kitchen than anywhere else with the exception of the MasterChef studios or behind the controls of the beloved airplane he shares with a syndicate of other would-be 'Biggles'. Franc Roddam, who thought up the programme, is married to a wonderful cook and is lucky enough to spend most of his kitchen time tasting. Our executive producer Brad Adams is gradually heading towards MasterChef status himself while Richard Kalms, our other executive producer, has a new baby and is really too tired to worry too much about what he eats! Associate Producer Glynis Robertson describes her cooking as learned at her mother's knee, but inspired by the series. Production co-ordinator Julie Dixon is our in-house vegetarian cook, whilst our other production co-ordinator Julia Park was a reserve contestant for MasterChef 1992. Towering above us all is our researcher Melanie Jappy who was a contestant on MasterChef 1991 and enjoyed the programme so much that she gave up the law and came to work with us for three years.

So if you were ever trapped in a log cabin in the mountains with any member of the Junior MasterChef team you would be sure to eat well. Aside from being excellent kitchen companions my colleagues all work like slaves to ensure that every one of our Junior Contestants has the time of their lives – albeit a sometimes nerve-wracking one – as they cook their way through our competition.

I regret to say that I could never have qualified as a Junior MasterChef contestant. I didn't attempt anything more adventurous than scrambled eggs until a miserable winter weekend in London when I immured myself in my flat with a couple of bags of groceries and a copy of the now sadly out-of-print Kitchen Primer by Craig Claibourne. By Sunday night there was more than scrambled eggs on the menu. I have never looked back and I only wish that I'd started twenty years earlier. There is no doubt in my mind at least that everyone should be able to cook. Even putting practical considerations aside, cooking is as exciting and uplifting as being able to play the piano, look intelligently at a painting or speak another language.

Throughout the series, it has been particularly gratifying to see that our young cooks aren't brattish prodigies or freaks or bores. They are enthusiastic, accomplished young people, full of fun and energy, who have not only inspired us and many viewers, but have also given us some jolly good ideas for our own kitchens as well. This book full of their delightful recipes is dedicated to the families of all our young cooks who encouraged, tasted, watched and waited. I thank them all.

Loyd Grossman

Notes for Recipe Users

Quantities are given in metric and imperial measures.
Follow one set of measurements only, not a combination,
because they are not interchangeable.

All spoon measures are level.

Fresh herbs are used unless otherwise stated.

Size 2 eggs are used unless otherwise suggested.

Ovens must be preheated to the temperature
specified in the recipe.

All recipes serve 2.

Introduction

From Aberdeen to the Channel Islands, from Truro to Norwich, once more we have gathered together, from the huge number of hopefuls, twenty-seven of the most talented young cooks in Britain to do battle in the red, yellow and blue kitchens for the honour of becoming the nation's Junior MasterChef.

But where did they all learn to cook? Most of our contestants have parents with a love of food. The mother of last year's Junior Master-Chef reached this year's MasterChef final, and two more juniors have mothers who have taken part in the senior contest with many a father threatening to try his hand. Other young cooks have found their way, between the hockey match and the maths homework, into professional kitchens to further their knowledge whilst washing the dishes. Some are still fortunate enough to have schools where Home Economics is taken seriously and the teacher's ambitions run to more than cheese scones.

Wherever they have acquired their skills, our contestants have once more amazed the judges with their imagination, flair and talent. Not everything has gone according to plan, but there has hardly been a damp eye in the kitchen despite the pressures of a strict ninety-minute time limit and seven cameras poking their lenses into everything whisked or stirred, peeled or puréed.

The recipes in this book will astound you. A significant number of our award winning guest chefs confess to having started cooking in their twenties. Yet some of the dishes you are about to enjoy have been calmly prepared under the glare of the television lights and whilst chatting away to the three judges... by ten year olds!

Richard Bryan
Producer and Director
Junior MasterChef

Contestants
Ben Domb • Oriyomi Abiola • Tom Slack

Panel of Judges
Ken Hom • Anthea Turner • Loyd Grossman

WINNER

Ben Domb's Menu

MAIN COURSE
"Raffles" style Spiced Chicken with Yogurt
Long Grain and Wild Rice with Pine Nuts and Walnuts
Mixed Leaf Salad
"I thought the chicken was absolutely fabulous" **Loyd**

DESSERT
Rose-fragrant Baklava
"It was outstanding" **Ken Hom**

Fifteen year old Ben Domb is from Child's Hill in North-west London. Ben is an extremely impressive juggler – of balls, clubs and even firebrands! Another of Ben's passions is animation, and with his recently acquired camera and tripod, he is now producing some pretty professional results. Ben also has a novel collection of phone cards, many of which are now rather valuable!

"RAFFLES" STYLE SPICED CHICKEN AND YOGURT

*2 chicken breast fillets, each about
150 g (5 oz)*

Marinade:
*2 lemon grass stalks, bruised
7.5 ml (1½ tsp) thick soy sauce
½ large onion, finely chopped
15 ml (1 tbsp) ground coriander
1 bunch of fresh coriander, trimmed
and chopped
7.5 ml (1½ tsp) ground cumin
1-2 garlic cloves, crushed
10 ml (2 tsp) sugar
salt, to taste
30 ml (2 tbsp) vinegar
5 ml (1 tsp) oil*

To Serve:
*45-60 ml (3-4 tbsp) yogurt
½ red pepper, seeded and cut into very
fine strips
coriander leaves, to garnish*

1 To make the marinade, mix all the ingredients together in a dish large enough to hold the chicken breasts in a single layer. Add the chicken and turn to coat. Leave to marinate in a cool place for about 1 hour.

2 Remove the chicken breasts from the marinade with a slotted spoon. Place on the grill rack and cook under a preheated moderate grill for about 15 minutes, turning once, until cooked through.

3 Cut into thick slices and arrange on warmed serving plates. Spoon the yogurt into the centre of the plate and garnish with pepper strips, and coriander. Serve with the Rice with Pine Nuts and Walnuts (see page 12), and a simple leafy salad.

LONG-GRAIN AND WILD RICE WITH PINE NUTS AND WALNUTS

15 ml (1 tbsp) oil
125 g (4 oz) long-grain rice
40 g (1½ oz) wild rice
25 g (1 oz) pine nuts (approximately)
25 g (1 oz) walnuts (approximately)

1 Heat the oil in a large pan, add the rice, pine nuts and walnuts and fry for 2-3 minutes, stirring.

2 Add enough water to cover the rice by about 2.5 cm (1 inch). Bring to the boil, then simmer for about 30 minutes, until the rice is tender but still retains a bite.

WILD RICE

Wild rice is not as the name suggests a type of rice but the seed of an aquatic grass. It is dark brown in colour and has a strong, nutty flavour. As it is relatively expensive wild rice is usually mixed with other grains or rice. Look out for commercially prepared mixtures.

ROSE-FRAGRANT BAKLAVA

110 g (3½ oz) butter, melted
225 g (8 oz) filo pastry (approximately
  12 sheets)
140 g (4½ oz) shelled pistachio nuts,
  coarsely chopped
30 ml (2 tbsp) caster sugar

Sugar Syrup:
125 g (4 oz) caster sugar
15-30 ml (1-2 tbsp) lemon juice
few drops of rose essence, to taste

To Decorate:
crystallised rose petals
pistachio nuts

1 First make the syrup. Place the sugar, lemon juice and 50 ml (2 fl oz) water in a pan and heat gently until the sugar has dissolved. Simmer for 1-2 minutes, then add the rose essence. Cool slightly, then chill.

2 Brush the bottom and sides of a 20 x 15 cm (8 x 6 inch) baking tin with melted butter. Lay one filo sheet in the tin and brush with butter. Lay another sheet over the top and brush with the butter. Layer half of the filo sheets in the tin in this way, brushing each sheet with butter as you lay it in. Sprinkle the nuts and sugar evenly over the pastry.

3 Cover with the rest of the filo sheets, brushing with butter as before. Brush the top sheet generously to finish. Using a very sharp knife, cut the pastry into diamonds or triangles. Bake in a preheated oven at 190°C (375°F) mark 5 for 20 minutes, then increase the temperature to 220°C (425°F) mark 7 and cook for a further 10-15 minutes, until very puffy and golden in colour.

4 Remove from the oven and immediately pour the chilled syrup over the baklava. Leave in the tin for about 1 hour until the syrup has been absorbed before serving. Decorate with crystallised rose petals and pistachio nuts.

Contestants

Ben Domb • Oriyomi Abiola • Tom Slack

Panel of Judges

Ken Hom • Anthea Turner • Loyd Grossman

Oriyomi Abiola's Menu

MAIN COURSE

Seafood Couscous, served with Poached Scottish Salmon

"The couscous was really very tasty... and the poached salmon was cooked to perfection" **Ken Hom**

DESSERT

Pears cooked in Red Wine, served with Zabaglione

"I liked the zabaglione" **Ken Hom**

Oriyomi Abiola, known as Yomi, is 12 years of age and lives in Swiss Cottage, North London. Yomi attends Queen's School in Harley Street, where modern dancing is probably her favourite subject. Yomi's latest passion is fencing and she is fortunate to have an Olympic fencer as her teacher.

SEAFOOD COUSCOUS WITH POACHED SCOTTISH SALMON

Couscous:
75 g (3 oz) couscous
2 small carrots, diced
75 ml (5 tbsp) frozen peas
75 ml (5 tbsp) frozen sweetcorn kernels
45 ml (3 tbsp) sunflower oil
1 fish or chicken stock cube
14 cooked king prawns
125 g (4 oz) cooked peeled prawns
pinch of mild curry powder
15 g (½ oz) butter
5 ml (1 tsp) light muscovado sugar
¼ red pepper, seeded and diced
¼ yellow pepper, seeded and diced

Salmon:
150 ml (¼ pint) dry white wine
30 ml (2 tbsp) olive oil
5 ml (1 tsp) lemon juice
sea salt
2 Scottish salmon cutlets, each
   150-175 g (5-6 oz)

To Garnish:
steamed and lightly buttered spinach
4 red pepper strips
lemon slices
dill and parsley sprigs

1 Place the couscous in a pressure cooker. Add approximately 250 ml (8 fl oz) water to just cover. Bring to high pressure and cook for 10 minutes, then reduce the pressure slowly; the couscous should be softened and have absorbed all of the water. Lightly fork through to separate the grains.

2 Meanwhile, blanch the carrots, peas and sweetcorn in boiling water for 5 minutes; drain.

3 Heat the oil in a frying pan, then add the stock cube and 90 ml (3 fl oz) water; stir to dissolve. Add all of the prawns and warm through gently. Remove the prawns; set aside the king prawns and the stock and keep warm.

4 Add the carrots, peas, sweetcorn and small prawns to the couscous and mix well. Season with salt and add enough curry powder to give a subtle flavour and a hint of colour.

5 Melt the butter in a small pan, add the sugar and heat gently until dissolved. Mix into the couscous, then stir in the diced peppers. Spoon into two 9 cm (3½ inch) ramekins; keep warm.

6 To poach the salmon, pour the wine into a shallow frying pan, add the oil and lemon juice and season with sea salt. Add the salmon cutlets to the pan and poach for 3 minutes on each side or until cooked.

7 Place a bed of spinach on each warmed serving plate, surround with two strips of red pepper, then top with a salmon cutlet. Garnish with lemon, dill and a few king prawns.

8 Pour the reserved stock on to a serving plate, turn the couscous out on top and arrange the remaining prawns around it. Garnish with parsley and serve with the salmon.

PEARS IN RED WINE WITH ZABAGLIONE

500 ml (16 fl oz) red wine
15 g (½ oz) sugar
2 cloves
½ vanilla pod
2 pears

Zabaglione:
2 egg yolks
25 g (1 oz) caster sugar
45 ml (3 tbsp) Marsala

To Decorate:
lemon slices

1 To cook the pears, put the wine in a saucepan, add the sugar, cloves and vanilla and stir gently until the sugar dissolves. Meanwhile, peel and core the pears. Add them to the pan and cook over a low heat for 20-25 minutes until tender, but not falling apart.

2 Meanwhile, make the zabaglione. Put the egg yolks in a heatproof bowl, add the sugar and Marsala and leave for a few minutes to settle.

3 Place the bowl over a pan of simmering water, making sure the base of the bowl doesn't touch the water. Using an electric whisk, whisk the mixture for about 10 minutes until it has substantially increased in volume and is the consistency of a thick cream.

4 Remove the poached pears from the syrup with a slotted spoon and place on warmed individual serving plates. Decorate with lemon slices. Spoon the zabaglione into warmed glasses and serve immediately, with the pears.

ZABAGLIONE

A classic Italian dessert, this frothy mixture of Marsala, egg yolks and sugar is served warm. Marsala is a Sicilian fortified wine available from larger supermarkets and wine merchants.

REGIONAL HEATS
London

Contestants
Ben Domb • Oriyomi Abiola • Tom Slack

Panel of Judges
Ken Hom • Anthea Turner • Loyd Grossman

Tom Slack's Menu

MAIN COURSE

Escalope of Veal, with a Sun-dried Tomato and Mushroom Stuffing, served with a Wine Cream Sauce

"The veal was really beautifully cooked, and I liked the stuffing" **Loyd**

DESSERT

Surprise Surprise!

"The dessert was out of this world... it was perfectly executed" **Loyd**

Fourteen year old Tom Slack comes from Charlton in South-east London. He is extremely keen on sailing and spends many a thrilling afternoon in a yacht battling with the elements. Boats of the past are also one of Tom's passions and he is a frequent visitor to the Cutty Sark. Tom also has an ever increasing collection of fossils and crystals.

STUFFED ESCALOPES OF VEAL WITH A WINE CREAM SAUCE

2 tomatoes
50 g (2 oz) butter
2 small onions, chopped
2 cloves garlic, chopped
25 g (1 oz) sun-dried tomatoes,
    chopped
75 g (3 oz) button mushrooms,
    chopped
salt and freshly ground black pepper
2 veal escalopes, each about 125 g
    (4 oz)
5 ml (1 tsp) capers, drained
125 g (4 oz) fresh spinach, trimmed
dash of white wine
60 ml (2 fl oz) veal stock
    (approximately)
60 ml (2 fl oz) double cream

To Garnish:
sautéed wild mushrooms

1 Place the tomatoes in a bowl, cover with boiling water and leave for about 1 minute. Remove from the water, slit and remove the skins, then dice the flesh to make a concasse; set aside.

2 Melt half the butter in a frying pan, add the onions, garlic, sun-dried tomatoes and mushrooms. Season with salt and pepper to taste and cook for 10 minutes.

3 Lay the veal escalopes out flat on a work surface and beat out thinly with a rolling pin or meat mallet. Spread with the cooked tomato mixture, then add the capers and salt and pepper to taste. Roll up and tie with string.

4 Melt the remaining butter in a pan, add the rolled escalopes and fry quickly, turning to seal and brown. Transfer to an ovenproof dish and cook in a preheated oven at 170°C (325°F) mark 3 for 5 minutes.

5 Meanwhile, cook the spinach with just the water clinging to the leaves after washing for about 5 minutes. Wrap the escalopes in buttered foil and leave in the switched-off oven to keep warm. Drain the spinach thoroughly.

6 Deglaze the frying pan with the wine and veal stock, then add the cream. Keep warm over a low heat.

7 Slice the veal into thick slices and arrange in a circle on warmed serving plates. Put any remaining stuffing in the middle and top with the spinach. Spoon the sauce around the veal and garnish with the tomato concasse and sautéed wild mushrooms.

SURPRISE SURPRISE!

Choux Pastry:
150 ml (¼ pint) water
40 g (1½ oz) butter
50 g (2 oz) plain flour, sifted
pinch of salt
2 eggs, beaten
beaten egg to glaze

Filling:
60 ml (2 fl oz) double cream
15 ml (1 tbsp) Calvados
60 ml (2 fl oz) apple purée
  (approximately)

To Finish:
25 g (1 oz) sugar
125 g (4 oz) blackberries
15 ml (1 tbsp) crème de cassis

1 To make the choux pastry, put the water and butter in a saucepan. Heat gently until melted, then bring to the boil. Remove from the heat and immediately tip in the flour and salt. Beat vigorously with a wooden spoon until the mixture is smooth and leaves the side of the pan clean. Slowly add the beaten eggs, until a smooth glossy paste is formed.

2 Using a large piping bag fitted with a 2.5 cm (1 inch) nozzle, pipe the pastry into two 10 cm (4 inch) lengths and two 2.5 cm (1 inch) rounds well apart on a dampened baking sheet. Glaze with beaten egg and bake in a preheated oven at 200°C (400°F) mark 6 for 20 minutes until well risen and golden. Leave to cool for 10 minutes in the switched-off oven.

3 Meanwhile, prepare the filling. Whip the cream with the Calvados until thick, then fold in the apple purée. Split the éclairs and fill with the mixture. Arrange on serving plates.

4 To finish, place the sugar and 45 ml (3 tbsp) water in a pan, dissolve over a low heat, then boil, without stirring, for 1 minute. Place the blackberries in a food processor, add the sugar syrup and crème de cassis and work to a purée. Pass through a fine sieve into a bowl. Pour the blackberry sauce around the éclairs to serve.

REGIONAL HEATS
The South West

Contestants
Jenna Tinson • Anya Barry • Teresa Penny

Panel of Judges
Ruth Rogers • Roger Black • Loyd Grossman

WINNER

Jenna Tinson's Menu

MAIN COURSE

Cornish Crab Pancakes with a Herb and Butter Sauce

Warm Carrot and Courgette Salad with a Lime Dressing

"I loved it – not just the crab filling – the pancakes were lovely too" **Roger Black**

DESSERT

Honey-poached Pears with a Plum and Cardamom Coulis, served with Almond Biscuits and Amaretto Cream

"That dessert was excellent" **Roger Black**

Twelve year old Jenna Tinson comes from Truro in Cornwall. She is an animal lover and is devoted to her border collie, named Sky. Jenna is particularly keen on riding, and makes light work of some pretty impressive jumps on her favourite pony, Ferdie. Jenna's other diverse interests include playing the grand piano and wind-surfing.

CORNISH CRAB PANCAKES WITH A HERB AND BUTTER SAUCE

Saffron Pancakes:
100 g (3½ oz) plain flour
½ sachet powdered saffron
2 eggs
200 ml (7 fl oz) milk
pinch of salt
25 g (1 oz) butter

Crab Filling:
15 g (½ oz) butter
1 spring onion, chopped
125 g (4 oz) ricotta cheese
225 g (8 oz) mixed brown and white
   crab meat
2 pinches of cayenne pepper
salt and freshly ground black pepper
freshly grated nutmeg
squeeze of lemon juice

Herb and Butter Sauce:
125 ml (4 fl oz) double cream
125 ml (4 fl oz) fish stock
15 ml (1 tbsp) butter
5 ml (1 tsp) chopped herbs (eg parsley,
   fennel), to taste

To Garnish:
parsley or fennel

COOK'S TIP

Saffron strands can be used instead of powdered saffron for the pancake batter. Heat the milk and water, add a pinch of saffron strands and leave to infuse until cool. Use the milk as above.

---

1 First make the pancakes. Sift the flour and saffron powder into a bowl. Make a well in the centre, add the eggs and whisk gently. Add the milk and 90 ml (3 fl oz) water a little at a time, beating constantly. Add the salt.

2 Heat the butter in a pan until melted and golden brown in colour, then immediately pour into the pancake batter.

3 Heat a pancake pan until really hot. Pour in enough batter to coat the base of the pan thinly and cook until golden brown underneath. Turn over and cook the other side, then slide it onto a warmed plate and keep warm while cooking the remaining batter in the same way, to make 4 pancakes in total.

4 To make the filling, melt the butter in a small pan, add the spring onion, cover and sweat gently for 1 minute.

5 Mix the ricotta and crab meat together in a bowl. Add the cayenne, salt, pepper and nutmeg to taste. Stir in the spring onion and a squeeze of lemon juice. Set aside.

6 To make the sauce, put the cream, stock and butter in a pan and whisk together over a low heat. Add salt and pepper and heat until slightly thickened, then add the chopped herbs.

7 To assemble, divide the filling between the pancakes and fold to enclose. Place 2 pancakes on each warmed plate and surround with the sauce. Garnish with parsley or fennel and serve at once, with the vegetables.

WARM CARROT AND COURGETTE SALAD WITH A LIME DRESSING

1 carrot
1 courgette
15 ml (1 tbsp) butter
5 ml (1 tsp) sugar
grated rind and juice of 1 lime

To Garnish:
5 ml (1 tsp) freshly chopped coriander

1 Slice the carrot and courgette into ribbons, using a swivel vegetable peeler.

2 Briefly blanch the carrot strips in boiling water until slightly softened. Drain and rinse under cold running water.

3 Melt the butter in a pan, add the carrot and courgette ribbons and sauté until tender.

4 Add the sugar, grated lime rind and juice and toss gently until glazed. Garnish with coriander to serve.

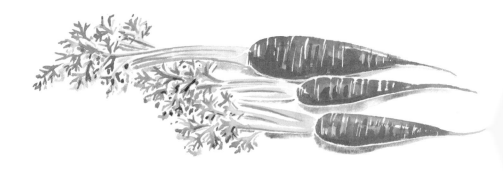

HONEY-POACHED PEARS WITH PLUM AND CARDAMOM COULIS

2 pears
45 ml (3 tbsp) clear honey

Plum and Cardamom Coulis:
575 g (1¼ lb) plums, halved and
  stoned
60 ml (2 fl oz) orange juice
30 ml (2 tbsp) clear honey
30 ml (2 tbsp) amaretto di Saronno
  liqueur
10 crushed cardamoms, tied in muslin

To Serve:
60 ml (2 fl oz) double cream
7.5 ml (1½ tsp) amaretto di Saronno
  liqueur
4 Almond Biscuits (see right)
icing sugar, for dusting

1 Peel the pears and cut in half length-ways. Place the honey in a pan with 250 ml (8 fl oz) water and heat gently until the honey has dissolved. Add the pears, cover and poach for about 10 minutes.

2 Meanwhile, put all the ingredients for the coulis in a pan, cover and simmer for 10 minutes, stirring occa-sionally. Take off the lid and cook until reduced a little. Leave to cool, then work in a food processor until smooth.

3 Whip the cream until thick, then fold in the liqueur. Chill until required.

4 To serve, place a biscuit on each serving plate, arrange 2 pear halves on top and cover with another biscuit. Pour the coulis around and add a spoonful of the cream. Dust with icing sugar and serve at once.

ALMOND BISCUITS

90 g (3¼ oz) soft butter
25 g (1 oz) icing sugar, sifted
25 g (1 oz) ground almonds
100 g (3½ oz) plain flour, sifted
1.25 ml (¼ tsp) almond essence

1 Place all the ingredients in a bowl and work together until evenly blended to form a firm paste.

2 Turn out onto a floured surface, knead lightly, then roll out carefully to a 5 mm (¼ inch) thickness. Cut out four 7.5 cm (3 inch) rounds and place on a baking sheet lined with non-stick baking parchment.

3 Bake in a preheated oven at 180°C (350°F) mark 4 for 8 minutes or until pale golden. Cool on a wire rack.

REGIONAL HEATS
The South West

Contestants
Jenna Tinson • Anya Barry • Teresa Penny

Panel of Judges
Ruth Rogers • Roger Black • Loyd Grossman

Anya Barry's Menu

MAIN COURSE

Mushroom and Ricotta Pasta Parcels, with a Tomato and Basil
Sauce, served with a Salad

"It was lovely" **Roger Black**

DESSERT

Elderflower Cream on a Pecan Biscuit Base with
a Blackcurrant Coulis

"That was a wonderful pudding" **Loyd**

Anya Barry from Bath is 13 years old and attends the
Ralph Allen School. She is a keen musician, both
playing the clarinet and singing. Anya's also a talented
dancer and has pirouetted her way to grade 4. To augment
her pocket money, Anya produces a range of brightly
coloured jewellery.

MUSHROOM AND RICOTTA PASTA PARCELS

Pasta:
100 g (3½ oz) strong white bread flour
salt and freshly ground black pepper
1 egg

Filling:
25 g (1 oz) butter
5 mushrooms, diced
1 clove garlic, crushed
5 ml (1 tsp) vegetable stock
22.5 ml (1½ tbsp) ricotta cheese
15 ml (1 tbsp) freshly grated Parmesan
  cheese
pinch of freshly grated nutmeg

Tomato and Basil Sauce:
15 ml (1 tbsp) olive oil
1 small onion, chopped
900 g (2 lb) ripe tomatoes, skinned and
  chopped
100 ml (3½ fl oz) red wine
15 ml (1 tbsp) tomato purée
10 ml (2 tbsp) brown sugar
2 basil sprigs, chopped

To Garnish:
freshly grated Parmesan cheese

1 To make the pasta, sift the flour and a pinch of salt into a mixing bowl. Make a well in the centre and add the egg. Using a wooden spoon, gradually mix the flour into the egg. When the mixture begins to thicken, mix in the rest of the flour with your hands, to make a moist but not sticky dough. If it is too sticky, add a little more flour. Divide the dough in half and knead lightly.

2 Pass the dough through a pasta machine on the widest setting. Fold the piece in half and feed it through again. Repeat this about 5 times on each setting, gradually narrowing the setting. Repeat with the other piece of dough. Keep covered to prevent drying out.

3 To prepare the filling, melt the butter in a frying pan, add the mushrooms and garlic and sauté for 2-3 minutes. Add the stock and cook on a medium heat for a few minutes. Mix well, then lower the heat and cook for 20-30 minutes, stirring occasionally.

4 To make the sauce, heat the olive oil in a large pan, add all the rest of the ingredients, except the basil, and simmer for 20 minutes. Purée in a blender or food processor, then pass through a sieve to remove the pips. Stir in the basil and seasoning to taste.

5 Transfer the mushrooms to a bowl, add the ricotta cheese and mix well, then sprinkle with the Parmesan cheese, and nutmeg, salt and pepper to taste.

6 Place one sheet of pasta on a work surface. Spoon heaped teaspoons of the filling at 6 cm (2½ inch) intervals along the strip. Using a pastry brush, lightly moisten the dough along the edges and between the filling with water. Cover with the remaining pasta, then press with your fingers along the edges and between the filling, to seal. Cut between the stuffing with a pastry cutter or sharp knife, and neaten the long edges. Alternatively, use a ravioli tin.

7 Cook the pasta in a large pan of boiling salted water for about 8 minutes, until the sealed edges are al dente. Drain thoroughly and transfer to a warmed serving dish. Pour on the sauce, sprinkle with Parmesan and serve at once.

ELDERFLOWER CREAMS

75 ml (5 tbsp) whipping cream
½ sachet of powdered gelatine
15 g (½ oz) caster sugar
75 ml (5 tbsp) Greek yogurt
45 ml (3 tbsp) elderflower cordial
  (approximately)

Pecan Biscuit Base:
4 Hobnob biscuits
25 g (1 oz) shelled pecan nuts,
  roughly chopped
50 g (2 oz) butter

Blackcurrant Coulis:
225 g (8 oz) blackcurrants
75 g (3 oz) caster sugar

To Decorate:
2 pecan nuts
5 ml (1 tsp) single cream

COOK'S TIP

If you have a food processor, place the biscuits and nuts in the bowl and work until fine crumbs form. Melt the butter, add to the processor bowl and work for a few seconds to combine.

---

1 Put 30 ml (2 tbsp) of the cream in a cup and sprinkle on the gelatine. Leave to soften for 10 minutes.

2 Meanwhile, put the rest of the cream into a pan, add the sugar and heat very gently until the sugar has dissolved. Add the soaked gelatine and whisk until it has dissolved and the mixture is smooth.

3 Pour the yogurt into a measuring jug, then add the elderflower cordial very slowly, to avoid curdling. Stir in the cream mixture, then pass through a sieve into a bowl. Give it a good stir and taste to check that the elderflower flavour is sufficient. If necessary, add a little more cordial. Return to the jug and stand in a bowl of iced water – this speeds up the setting time.

4 Meanwhile, prepare the pecan biscuit base. Crumble the biscuits into a strong greaseproof paper bag, add the pecans then crush with a rolling pin to make crumbs.

5 Melt the butter in a pan, add the crumb mixture and mix well. Press onto the base of two 10 cm (4 inch) individual flan dishes and chill until firm.

6 To make the coulis, place the blackcurrants and sugar in a bowl, mix until slightly 'mushy', then leave to stand for 30 minutes. Strain through a nylon sieve.

7 When the cream mixture is on the point of setting, spoon on top of the biscuit base. Return to the refrigerator for about 1 hour, until set. Place on a serving plate and top with a pecan nut. Pour the blackcurrant coulis around, dot with the cream and use a cocktail stick to feather out.

REGIONAL HEATS
The South West

Contestants
Jenna Tinson • Anya Barry • Teresa Penny

Panel of Judges
Ruth Rogers • Roger Black • Loyd Grossman

Teresa Penny's Menu

MAIN COURSE
Fillet of Scottish Wild Salmon with Rhubarb Sauce
Steamed Carrots, Mangetouts and Baby Corn
New Potatoes

DESSERT
Apple and Thyme Sponge Pudding with Toffee Sauce
"An amazing pudding" **Loyd**

Teresa Penny from Bournemouth is 13 years old. She is a proud member of the Highcliffe Junior Choir, which performs throughout Britain and has taken part in a Prom concert at the Royal Albert Hall. Teresa has also recently started trampolining. With sister Katherine and brother Geoffrey, Teresa runs a small business – producing wonderful things out of salt dough, which they sell at the local car boot sale!

FILLET OF SCOTTISH WILD SALMON WITH RHUBARB SAUCE

2 filleted salmon cutlets, each 150 g (5 oz)
½ carrot, cut into julienne
1 celery stalk, cut into julienne
¼ onion, finely chopped
few broccoli stalks, finely diced
¼ lemon
salt and freshly ground black pepper
2 knobs of butter

Rhubarb Sauce:

20 g (¾ oz) butter
60 g (2½ oz) rhubarb, chopped
125 ml (4 fl oz) double cream

To Garnish:

dill sprigs

1 Butter 2 large squares of foil. Separate each of the boneless salmon cutlets into 2 pieces. Divide the carrot, celery, onion and broccoli equally between the foil and place the salmon on top. Place a slice of lemon on each salmon piece, squeeze on a little extra lemon juice and season well with salt and pepper. Add a knob of butter, then fold the foil loosely around the salmon to seal it completely.

2 Place the parcels on a baking sheet and cook in a preheated oven at 180°C (350°F) mark 4 for 15 minutes.

3 Meanwhile, prepare the sauce. Place the butter in a pan, add 50 ml (2 fl oz) water and heat until melted. Add the rhubarb with salt and pepper to taste and cook gently until the water has evaporated and the rhubarb is soft. Pass the rhubarb through a nylon sieve into a bowl, then return to the pan and stir in the cream. Heat gently until slightly thickened.

4 To serve, open the salmon parcels, being careful of the steam. Transfer the salmon to warmed serving plates, carefully removing and discarding the vegetables. Garnish with dill and serve with the sauce. Accompany with steamed carrots, mangetouts, baby corn and new potatoes.

APPLE AND THYME SPONGE WITH TOFFEE SAUCE

caster sugar, for sprinkling
1 Cox's apple, about 115 g (4 oz)
20 g (¾ oz) unsalted butter
3 ml (½ tsp) chopped thyme
15 ml (1 tbsp) soft light brown sugar
1 egg, separated
20 g (¾ oz) vanilla sugar (see below)
pinch of salt
30 g (1¼ oz) self-raising flour
125 ml (4 fl oz) whipping cream
1.25 ml (¼ tsp) finely grated lemon rind
5 ml (1 tsp) Grand Marnier or other
   orange-flavoured liqueur

Toffee Sauce:
55 g (2¼ oz) unsalted butter
55 g (2¼ oz) soft brown sugar
30 ml (2 tbsp) single cream

To Finish:
icing sugar, for dusting

VANILLA SUGAR

To make your own vanilla sugar, simply keep a vanilla pod immersed in a jar of caster sugar to impart flavour.

1 Grease two ramekins, 9 cm (3½ inches) in diameter with butter, then sprinkle with caster sugar to coat. Peel and core the apple and cut into 16 slices. Melt the butter in a frying pan, add the apple and half of the thyme and cook for 1 minute, stirring. Sprinkle with the brown sugar and cook for 5 minutes until soft. Add 15 ml (1 tbsp) water, simmer to reduce, then transfer the apples to a plate and drain well.

2 Whisk the egg yolk and vanilla sugar together until pale. Add the salt, flour and whipping cream and whisk until smooth. Stir in the lemon rind and Grand Marnier. Whisk the egg white in a bowl until soft peaks form, then fold into the cream mixture.

3 Place a small amount of the mixture in each ramekin, just enough to cover the base. Arrange 4 apple slices around the edge of each ramekin and sprinkle with the remaining thyme. Cover the apples with the remaining mixture, to 1 cm (½ inch) below the top of each ramekin. Bake in a preheated oven at 180°C (350°F) mark 4 for 20 minutes.

4 Meanwhile, make the sauce. Place all the ingredients in a small pan and slowly bring to the boil, stirring. Cook for about 2 minutes, until smooth.

5 Remove the sponges from the ramekins and place on 2 serving plates. Decorate with the remaining apple slices and sprinkle with icing sugar. Serve with the toffee sauce.

Contestants
Robyn Hardy • Ward Burkhill • Jill Lewis

Panel of Judges
Jean Christophe Novelli • Sarah Greene • Loyd Grossman

WINNER

Robyn Hardy's Menu

MAIN COURSE
Seafood Crêpes
Julienne of Carrots and Baby Courgettes tossed in butter
"I liked the seafood filling very much" **Loyd**

DESSERT
Lemon Ice Cream in a Chocolate Basket
"Clean, simple, and extremely light. Cold, crunchy...
it was perfect" **Jean Christophe Novelli**

Robyn Hardy is twelve years old and comes from Cheadle in Cheshire. Robyn attends Withington Girls School, where she is a stalwart member of the Pets Club – the home to an unlikely combination of hamsters and stick insects! Robyn and her father are keen on kite flying, and have an impressive collection of kites. Robyn's other interests include riding.

SEAFOOD CRÊPES

Court Bouillon:

600 ml (1 pint) water mixed with white
  wine
15 ml (1 tbsp) lemon juice
½ carrot, chopped
1 small onion, chopped
½ celery stalk, chopped
1 bouquet garni
3 black peppercorns
1 teaspoon salt

Fish Filling:

1 small piece of cod
1 small piece of smoked haddock
100 g (3½ oz) cooked peeled prawns
25 g (1 oz) butter
25 g (1 oz) plain flour
chopped dill, to taste

Pancakes:

25 g (1 oz) buckwheat flour
75 g (3 oz) plain flour
5 ml (1 tsp) salt
1 egg
150 ml (¼ pint) milk
15 ml (1 tbsp) oil

To Finish:

25 g (1 oz) Cheddar cheese, grated
2 dill sprigs

1 To make the court bouillon, put all the ingredients in a pan, bring to the boil, then reduce the heat and simmer for 30 minutes. Remove from the heat and strain.

2 To prepare the filling, return the court bouillon to the pan and bring to the boil. Add the cod, lower the heat and simmer for 12 minutes.

3 Meanwhile, place the haddock in a dish. Cover with cling film and prick a

few holes, then microwave on high for 4 minutes.

4 Remove the cod from the pan, reserving the liquid. Flake both fish into a bowl, add the prawns and place in a very low oven to keep warm.

5 Melt the butter in a pan, stir in the flour and cook, stirring, for 1 minute to make a roux. Remove from the heat and gradually stir in 300 ml (½ pint) of the reserved court bouillon. Return to the heat and bring to the boil, stirring, until thickened. Season with chopped dill to taste. Pour over the fish and put back in the oven.

6 To make the pancakes, put the flours and salt in a bowl and stir to mix. Make a well in the centre and add the egg. Slowly blend the egg into the flour, then gradually add the milk and 150 ml (¼ pint) water. Add the oil and whisk well, until smooth.

7 Heat a non-stick frying pan and brush lightly with oil. Add a tablespoon of the batter and cook until lightly browned underneath, then turn and cook the other side. Transfer to a baking sheet, cover with foil and keep warm in the oven, while making 3 more pancakes.

8 To serve, divide the filling between the pancakes and fold in half to enclose. Sprinkle with the cheese and grill briefly until melted.

9 Serve with carrots and baby courgettes, cut into julienne and cooked lightly in melted butter.

LEMON ICE CREAM IN A CHOCOLATE BASKET

grated rind and juice of 3 large lemons
175 g (6 oz) caster sugar
2 egg whites
125 g (4 oz) plain chocolate, melted
300 ml (½ pint) double cream
300 ml (½ pint) Greek yogurt

1 Place the lemon rind and juice, sugar and 150 ml (¼ pint) water in a pan and bring slowly to the boil. Reduce the heat and simmer for 5 minutes. Whisk the egg whites in a bowl until they stand in peaks, then whisk in the hot syrup. Leave to cool.

2 Put the chocolate into a greaseproof piping bag fitted with a fine plain nozzle. Blow up 2 small round balloons until they are the required size and stand in 2 egg cups or glasses. Grease the balloons well. Pipe a lattice shape of chocolate over the top half of the balloons. Place in the freezer until solid.

3 When the ice cream mixture is cool, stir in the cream and yogurt and churn in an ice-cream maker for about 20 minutes.

4 When the chocolate is firm, burst the balloons. Leave for a moment, and the balloon should drop away from the chocolate.

5 Scoop the ice cream into balls and arrange on individual serving plates. Lay the chocolate lattice over the top.

Contestants

Robyn Hardy • Ward Burkhill • Jill Lewis

Panel of Judges

Jean Christophe Novelli • Sarah Greene • Loyd Grossman

Ward Burkhill's Menu

MAIN COURSE

Pan-fried Breast of Pigeon with Gratin Dauphinoise

"I loved the flavour and texture of the pigeon" **Sarah Greene**

DESSERT

Warm Chocolate Suchard with Honey Ice Cream

"The dessert was sublime" **Sarah Greene**

Fifteen year old Ward Burkhill comes from Winteringham near Scunthorpe. Ward attends Winteringham Comprehensive School, where he is a staunch member of the rugby team. Ward is also keen on clay pigeon shooting and fishing.

PAN-FRIED BREAST OF PIGEON

6 pigeon breasts
salt and freshly ground black pepper
25 g (1 oz) butter
6 crab apples
30 g (1¼ oz) sugar

Sauce:
600 ml (1 pint) well-flavoured pigeon
* stock*

1 First prepare the sauce. Simmer the stock in a saucepan until well reduced – to about 150 ml (¼ pint).

2 Meanwhile, dissolve the sugar in about 120 ml (4 fl oz) water in a pan over a low heat. Score the skin on the apples, place in the sugar syrup and bring to the boil. Simmer for 10 minutes, while cooking the pigeon.

3 Season the pigeon breasts with salt and pepper to taste. Place a heavy-based pan over a high heat. When it is very hot, add the butter. When the butter is sizzling hot, add the pigeon breasts and cook for 1-2 minutes on each side, or to taste.

4 Remove the pigeon breasts from the pan, slice thickly and arrange on a warmed serving plate. Surround with the crab apples and sauce. Accompany with the Gratin Dauphinoise.

GRATIN DAUPHINOISE

3 potatoes, sliced
450 ml (¾ pint) milk
1 clove garlic
salt and freshly ground black pepper
freshly grated nutmeg
30 ml (2 tbsp) double cream

1 Carefully arrange the potatoes in layers in an ovenproof dish. Pour on the milk, then crush the garlic over the surface and sprinkle with salt, pepper and nutmeg to taste. Bring to the boil, then reduce the heat and simmer for 10 minutes.

2 Pour the cream over the top, then cook in a preheated oven at 220°C (425°F) mark 7 for 20 minutes.

CHOCOLATE SUCHARD WITH HONEY ICE CREAM

250 g (9 oz) unsalted butter
250 g (9 oz) caster sugar
250 g (9 oz) plain chocolate, melted
8 egg yolks
25 g (1 oz) butter or margarine
100 g (3½ oz) ground almonds
5 egg whites
icing sugar, for dusting

1 Cream the unsalted butter and half of the sugar together in a bowl. Place over a pan of simmering water to warm slightly, then remove and add the chocolate; stir well until evenly mixed. Stir in the egg yolks, one at a time.

2 Rub the butter or margarine into the ground almonds then beat in the chocolate mixture.

3 Whisk the egg whites until stiff, then gradually whisk in the remaining sugar. Stir a third into the chocolate mixture to lighten it, then lightly fold in the rest. Transfer the mixture to an ovenproof dish and cook in a preheated oven at 140°C (275°F) mark 1 for 20-25 minutes, until firm. Turn out onto a serving plate and sprinkle with icing sugar. Decorate the plate with piped chocolate square lattices, if wished, and serve with the ice cream.   (Serves 4-6)

HONEY ICE CREAM

12 egg yolks
250 g (9 oz) caster sugar
500 ml (16 fl oz) milk
500 ml (16 fl oz) double cream
30 ml (2 tbsp) thin honey

1 Place the egg yolks and sugar in a bowl and beat until pale yellow. Put the milk and cream in a pan and bring to the boil. Add to the egg mixture, half at a time. Place over a pan of simmering water and whisk until the mixture coats the back of a wooden spoon. Whisk in the honey.

2 Place the mixture in an ice-cream maker and churn for about 50 minutes, then transfer to a suitable container and place in the freezer until required. If you do not have an ice cream machine, freeze the mixture in a shallow container, whisking occasionally to break down the ice crystals and ensure a smooth-textured result. (Serves 4-6)

COOK'S TIP

For an extra special effect, decorate each plate with a piped chocolate lattice. Use a greaseproof paper piping bag fitted with a plain nozzle to pipe melted chocolate onto non-stick baking parchment to form a lattice. Leave until set, then carefully peel off the paper.

Contestants

Robyn Hardy • Ward Burkhill • Jill Lewis

Panel of Judges

Jean Christophe Novelli • Sarah Greene • Loyd Grossman

Jill Lewis' Menu

MAIN COURSE

Chicken and Stilton Roulades

Carrots in Lemon Cream Sauce

Château Potatoes

"Very good. The stilton and bacon lend quite a powerful flavour" **Jean Christophe Novelli**

DESSERT

Larni Pudding

Thirteen year old Jill Lewis comes from Sunderland. A keen musician, Jill is currently taking lessons on the electronic keyboard. She also enjoys acting and has a role as 'The Cook' in the local church's theatrical production of Snow White. Jill is also an enthusiastic Guide and often helps her mother, who runs a Brownie Pack, to teach the Brownies needlework and embroidery.

CHICKEN AND STILTON ROULADES

50 g (2 oz) Stilton cheese, derinded
  and crumbled
75 g (3 oz) butter, softened
2 chicken breasts, each 150 g (5 oz),
  skinned and boned
4 rashers of smoked back bacon,
  derinded
15 ml (1 tbsp) vegetable oil
1 glass of red wine made up to 300 ml
  (½ pint) with chicken stock (see
  below)
salt and freshly ground black pepper
5 ml (1 tsp) arrowroot

To Garnish:
watercress sprigs
fried bread triangles

1 Place the cheese and 40 g (1½ oz) of the butter in a bowl and beat to form a smooth paste.

2 Lay the chicken breasts between two sheets of dampened greaseproof paper and beat with a rolling pin to flatten. Spread the butter mixture evenly over the top of each breast. Roll up the breasts, wrap in the bacon rashers and secure with wooden cocktail sticks.

3 Heat the oil and the remaining butter in a heavy-based pan, add the chicken breasts and brown well. Pour in the wine and stock and season with salt and pepper. Bring to the boil, then cover and simmer gently for 35-40 minutes, turning occasionally. Remove the cocktail sticks, place the chicken in a warmed serving dish and keep warm.

4 Blend the arrowroot with a little water until smooth. Pour into the pan juices and heat, stirring, until thickened. Season with salt and pepper to taste and spoon over the chicken. Garnish with watercress sprigs and fried bread triangles. Serve at once.

CHICKEN STOCK

Heat 15 ml (1 tbsp) oil in a pan, add the chicken bones, 1 chopped onion, 1 chopped leek and 2 chopped carrots; sauté until browned. Add a bouquet garni, salt and pepper and 600 ml (1 pint) water. Bring to the boil, then simmer for 1½ hours. Strain the stock before use.

CARROTS IN LEMON CREAM SAUCE

25 g (1 oz) butter
225 g (8 oz) carrots, thinly sliced
juice of ¼ lemon
freshly grated nutmeg, to taste
25 g (1 oz) sultanas
75 ml (5 tbsp) soured cream
salt and freshly ground black pepper
parsley sprigs, to garnish

1 Melt the butter in a pan, add the carrots, cover and cook gently for about 20 minutes, until just tender, shaking the pan occasionally to prevent sticking.

2 Stir in the lemon juice, nutmeg, sultanas and soured cream, season with salt and pepper to taste and heat through gently. Garnish with parsley to serve.

CHÂTEAU POTATOES

*450 g (1 lb) small new potatoes,
  scraped*
25 g (1 oz) butter
salt and freshly ground black pepper
parsley sprigs, to garnish

1 Cook the potatoes in boiling water for 5 minutes, drain well, then dry on kitchen paper.

2 Melt the butter in a shallow flame-proof casserole, add the potatoes and fry gently until golden brown on all sides. Season with salt and pepper, cover and cook in a preheated oven at 180°C (350°F) mark 4 for 20-25 minutes, until tender. Garnish with parsley to serve.

LARNI PUDDING

75 g (3 oz) caster sugar
200 g (7 oz) butter
50 g (2 oz) plain flour, sifted
pinch of salt
25 g (1 oz) flaked almonds
225 g (8 oz) icing sugar
5 ml (1 tsp) vanilla essence
4 egg yolks
1 kiwi fruit, peeled and cut into small
   pieces
1 pear, peeled and cut into small pieces
300 ml (½ pint) double cream, whipped

To Decorate:
flaked almonds
1 kiwi fruit, peeled and sliced

1 Place the caster sugar and 75 g (3 oz) of the butter in a bowl and beat until light and fluffy. Stir in the flour, salt and almonds.

2 Put teaspoons of the mixture, well spaced apart, on a greased baking sheet and flatten each with a wet fork. Bake in a preheated oven at 200°C (400°F) mark 6 for 5-6 minutes or until just coloured at the edges. Transfer to a wire rack to cool, then crush into small pieces with a rolling pin.

3 Put the crushed biscuits in a small glass serving bowl or 2 individual ones.

4 Place the remaining butter, icing sugar and vanilla essence in a bowl and beat until fluffy. Beat in the egg yolks, then add the chopped kiwi fruit and stir well. Spread the mixture over the biscuit crumbs.

5 Add the chopped pear to the whipped cream and spread over the butter mixture. Chill for 45 minutes.

6 Decorate with flaked almonds and sliced kiwi fruit to serve.

Wales

Contestants

Jenny Smith • Jenny Church • Helen Lunt

Panel of Judges

Christopher Chown • Frances Edmonds • Loyd Grossman

WINNER

Jenny Smith's Menu

MAIN COURSE

Cheese, Tomato and Mustard French Tart
Piedmont Peppers
Green Salad with Redcurrant Dressing
"Brilliantly executed" **Frances Edmonds**

DESSERT

Lemon and Cider Syllabub with Raspberries
"It was absolutely lovely that... it just zapped!" **Christopher Chown**

Fourteen year old Jenny Smith from Swansea is a pupil at Cwmtawe Comprehensive School. Jenny plays the saxophone in the school orchestra, which is renowned for its inspired performances. She plays in the school netball team too. Jenny is also a member of the school drama group which has a strong tradition of exciting musicals.

CHEESE, TOMATO AND MUSTARD TART

175 g (6 oz) puff pastry, thawed if frozen
5 ml (1 tsp) English mustard
7.5 ml (1½ tsp) French mustard
75-125 g (3-4 oz) Gouda cheese, thinly sliced
4 tomatoes, thickly sliced

1 Roll out the pastry on a floured surface and use to line a 20 cm (8 inch) square tin. Mix the mustards together and spread over the base of the pastry. Chill in the refrigerator for about 10 minutes.

2 Arrange the cheese slices in the pastry case in one layer. Arrange the tomato slices neatly on top.

3 Bake on the top shelf of a preheated oven at 200°C (400°F) mark 6 for about 30 minutes until golden and well risen.

4 Serve, cut into slices, accompanied by the Piedmont Peppers and salad (see page 43).

GREEN SALAD WITH REDCURRANT DRESSING

selection of salad leaves (eg rocket, little Gem lettuce, lamb's lettuce)

Redcurrant Dressing:
5 ml (1 tsp) redcurrant jelly (homemade if possible)
10 ml (2 tsp) red wine vinegar
10 ml (2 tsp) olive oil
pinch of chopped fresh mixed herbs
salt and freshly ground black pepper

1 Prepare the salad leaves and place in a salad bowl. Combine the dressing ingredients in a screw-topped jar and shake vigorously to combine. Pour over the salad leaves and toss lightly.

PIEDMONT PEPPERS

1 large red pepper
2 tomatoes, skinned and quartered
3 anchovy fillets
1 clove garlic, thinly sliced
15 ml (1 tbsp) olive oil
freshly ground black pepper

To Garnish:
basil leaves
black olives

1 Cut the pepper in half through the stalk and deseed. Place cut-side up in a shallow roasting dish. Fill with the tomato quarters.

2 Snip the anchovies into pieces and scatter over the tomatoes, with the garlic. Drizzle over the oil and season with pepper to taste.

3 Bake in a preheated oven at 180°C (350°F) mark 4 for about 1 hour, until soft. Garnish with basil and black olives to serve.

LEMON CIDER SYLLABUB WITH RASPBERRIES

125 g (4 oz) raspberries (thawed if
  frozen)
50 g (2 oz) caster sugar
75 ml (5 tbsp) sweet cider
finely grated rind of 1 lemon
juice of ½ lemon
150 ml (¼ pint) double cream

To Decorate:
mint leaves

1 Set aside 2 raspberries for decoration. Put the rest into a bowl and sprinkle with half of the sugar.

2 Place the cider, remaining sugar, lemon rind and juice in a bowl and beat well to combine. Gradually stir in the cream, then beat slowly and steadily until it forms soft peaks.

3 Divide the sugared raspberries between 2 wine glasses. Spoon the syllabub on top. Decorate with the reserved raspberries and mint leaves.

Wales

Contestants

Jenny Smith • Jenny Church • Helen Lunt

Panel of Judges

Christopher Chown • Frances Edmonds • Loyd Grossman

Jenny Church's Menu

MAIN COURSE

Duck Breast with Tarragon and Madeira Sauce

Puy Lentils with Wild Mushrooms

Sautéed Courgettes and Carrot Slices

"An excellent idea, the breast of duck with tarragon
and Madeira" **Frances Edmonds**

Dragon's Nest

"It was utterly brilliant... a really yummy chocolate pudding" **Christopher Chown**

Jenny Church is thirteen years old and comes from
Cardiff. Jenny has learnt many of her cookery skills
from her mother, Kerry, who was a MasterChef semi-
finalist in 1993. She's also very good at computing. Jenny
is a keen Guide and enjoys camping. She also has a
huge collection of frogs – china frogs, fluffy
frogs, paper frogs, etc!

DUCK BREAST WITH TARRAGON AND MADEIRA SAUCE

2 boneless duck breasts, each about
   175 g (6 oz)
salt and freshly ground black pepper
80 ml (6 tbsp) Madeira
30 ml (2 tbsp) red wine vinegar
150 ml (¼ pint) duck stock
15 g (½ oz) tarragon sprigs, chopped

1 Prick the duck breasts well and sprinkle with a little salt. Cook in a preheated oven at 220°C (425°F) mark 7 for 15 to 20 minutes, until the juices run clear when pierced with a skewer.

2 Meanwhile, mix the Madeira, wine vinegar and stock together in a pan, bring to the boil and boil until reduced slightly. Add the chopped tarragon and cook for a further 5 minutes. Check the seasoning.

3 Carve the duck breasts into thick slices, arrange on warmed serving plates and surround with the sauce. Serve with Puy Lentils with Wild Mushrooms (see page 47) and sautéed courgette and carrot slices.

PUY LENTILS WITH WILD MUSHROOMS

125 g (4 oz) Puy lentils
125 g (4 oz) wild mushrooms
15 g (½ oz) fresh parsley, chopped
15 g (½ oz) fresh thyme, chopped
1 small onion, finely chopped

1 Put the lentils, mushrooms, herbs and onion in a pan. Add 300 ml (½ pint) water, bring to the boil and boil for 5 minutes.

2 Reduce the heat and cook for 20 minutes or until the lentils are tender. Drain if necessary and season with salt and pepper to taste.

COOK'S TIP

If wild mushrooms are unobtainable, use 15 g (½ oz) dried mushrooms. Reconstitute them first by soaking in 300 ml (½ pint) warm water for about 20 minutes.

DRAGON'S NEST

50 g (2 oz) plain chocolate
10 ml (2 tsp) dark rum
50 g (2 oz) white chocolate
10 ml (2 tsp) kirsch
50 g (2 oz) butter
50 g (2 oz) caster sugar
2 eggs, separated
2 amaretti biscuits, crushed

To Finish:

50 g (2 oz) plain chocolate, melted
6 pitted bottled (or fresh) cherries

1 Place the plain chocolate and rum in one small bowl and the white chocolate and kirsch in another bowl. Heat both over a pan of simmering water until melted, then beat separately until smooth. Leave to cool slightly.

2 Place the butter and sugar in a bowl and beat until light and fluffy. Beat in the egg yolks, then divide the mixture in half.

3 Add the plain chocolate mixture to one half and the light chocolate to the other. Beat well.

4 Whisk the egg whites until they form peaks, then fold half into each mixture. Put a layer of amaretti crumbs in each of 2 sundae glasses. Cover with the plain chocolate mousse, then top with the white chocolate mousse. Chill in the refrigerator until set.

5 To finish, pour the melted chocolate onto a chopping board or marble slab. Spread into a thin layer with a palette knife, then leave until set. Using a sharp, thin-bladed knife, at a slight angle, push it across the chocolate with a slight sawing movement to make long scrolls.

6 Arrange chocolate scrolls on the white mousse around the edge of the dish, to form a 'nest' and place 3 cherry 'eggs' in the centre.

Wales

Contestants

Jenny Smith • Jenny Church • Helen Lunt

Panel of Judges

Christopher Chown • Frances Edmonds • Loyd Grossman

Helen Lunt's Menu

MAIN COURSE

Noisette of Welsh Lamb topped with a Basil Mousse, served on a Potato Rösti

Selection of Baby Vegetables

"The basil mousse was a nice idea, and it looked good" **Christopher Chown**

DESSERT

Bara Brith Ice Cream, served with a Mixed Fruit Cluster, a Raspberry Coulis and Langues de Chat

"The bara brith ice cream was excellent" **Christopher Chown**

Thirteen year old Helen Lunt comes from Howarden in Deeside. Helen is a green belt in the defensive art of Karate. She's also something of a Harley Davidson fanatic! On Saturdays, Helen earns her pocket money by helping the local butcher to make his highly prized and utterly delicious sausages.

NOISETTE OF WELSH LAMB TOPPED WITH BASIL MOUSSE ON A POTATO RÖSTI

1 chicken breast fillet, weighing about
175 g (6 oz), roughly chopped
leaves from 1 basil plant (about 35)
1½ egg whites
salt and freshly ground black pepper
45 ml (3 tbsp) double cream
2 noisettes of Welsh lamb
crepinette (caul fat), for wrapping

Potato Rösti:

2 large baking potatoes, grated
25 g (1 oz) clarified butter (see below)
75 ml (5 tbsp) oil

1 Put the chicken in a food processor and work until finely chopped. Add the basil, egg whites, salt, pepper and cream and work until smooth. Transfer to a bowl and chill until required.

2 Heat a heavy-based pan until very hot. Add the lamb and seal quickly on both sides. Place in a clean tea-towel until cool, then chill in the refrigerator for 5 minutes.

3 Spoon the prepared mousse onto one side of each noisette. Cover with crepinette, with the join underneath. Return to the hot pan to seal, then transfer to a foil-lined baking sheet and cook in a preheated oven at 180°C (350°F) mark 4 for 10-13 minutes.

4 Mix the grated potato and clarified butter together in a bowl, seasoning to taste with salt and pepper.

5 Heat the oil in 2 frying pans, add half of the potato to each and quickly spread out thinly into a round. Cook on both sides until browned, then transfer to warmed serving plates. Arrange the lamb on top and serve with steamed baby corn, carrots and mangetouts.

CLARIFIED BUTTER

This can be heated to a higher temperature than ordinary butter without burning. To prepare, melt the butter in a pan over a low heat, then skim the froth from the surface. Remove from the heat and allow to stand until sediment settles on the base of the pan. Carefully pour the clarified butter into a bowl, leaving the sediment behind.

BARA BRITH ICE CREAM WITH A MIXED FRUIT CLUSTER AND RASPBERRY COULIS

Ice Cream:
1 Bara Brith, broken into pieces
2 egg yolks
50 g (2 oz) caster sugar
150 ml (¼ pint) double cream
1 vanilla pod

Fruit Cluster:
1 kiwi fruit
½ banana
4 strawberries
squeeze of lemon juice

Raspberry Coulis:
125 g (4 oz) raspberries
25 g (1 oz) icing sugar
squeeze of lemon juice

To Serve:
Langues de Chat (see page 52)

1 Place the Bara Brith in a food processor and work until fine crumbs form.

2 Mix the egg yolks and caster sugar together in a bowl. Put the cream and vanilla pod in a pan and heat gently for about 1½ minutes. Add to the egg yolk mixture, stirring well. Transfer to an ice-cream machine and add the crumbs. Churn until firm, then transfer to 2 ramekins and freeze until firm.

3 Dice the kiwi fruit, banana and strawberries into 5 mm (¼ inch) pieces and mix with a little lemon juice. Spoon the fruit into 2 small ramekins, squashing down well, then chill until required.

4 To make the raspberry coulis, rub the raspberries through a nylon sieve into a bowl. Add the icing sugar and lemon juice to taste.

5 Scoop the ice cream onto serving plates, surround with the raspberry coulis and serve with the chilled fruit and Langues de Chat.

LANGUES DE CHAT

75 g (3 oz) unsalted butter
75 g (3 oz) caster sugar
3 egg whites
75 g (3 oz) plain flour
22.5 ml (1½ tbsp) cocoa powder
  (approximately)

1 To make the langues de chat, place the butter and sugar in a bowl and whisk until light and fluffy. Whisk in the egg whites, then whisk in the flour. Place one heaped spoonful of the mixture in another bowl and mix in the cocoa powder.

2 Spread the plain mixture thinly into claw shapes or rounds on a baking sheet lined with non-stick parchment, spacing them well apart. Pipe the cocoa mixture in lines over each one.

3 Bake in a preheated oven at 180°C (350°F) mark 4 for about 7 minutes, until golden.

4 Immediately lay each biscuit over a greased rolling pin so that it will curve as it cools. When set, carefully lift off the rolling pin and place on a wire rack to cool.

— The South East & Channel Isles—

Contestants

Cathy Merrick • Joanna Bruce • Rachel de Caen

Panel of Judges

Sue Lawrence • Rick Wakeman • Loyd Grossman

WINNER

Cathy Merrick's Menu

MAIN COURSE

Fillet of Venison with Mushroom Stuffing, and a Drambuie and Heather Honey Sauce

Celeriac Game Chips

Baby Leeks in Thyme Butter

"I thought that main course was just fabulous" **Sue Lawrence**

DESSERT

Cranberry and Clementine Sorbet

Autumn Leaf Biscuits

"The sorbet was perfect" **Loyd**

Cathy Merrick from Woodingdean, near Brighton, is fifteen years of age. Cathy attends Brighton & Hove High School where chemistry is probably her favourite subject. At home her hobbies include breeding guinea pigs. Cathy is also something of an expert at sugarcraft, and she often decorates celebration cakes for her family and friends.

VENISON WITH A MUSHROOM STUFFING, AND A DRAMBUIE AND HEATHER HONEY SAUCE

300 g (10 oz) fillet of venison
30 ml (2 tbsp) oil
2-3 rashers smoked streaky bacon, derinded

Marinade:
30 ml (2 tbsp) Drambuie
30 ml (2 tbsp) balsamic vinegar
7.5 ml (1½ tsp) heather honey
6 juniper berries, crushed
1 bay leaf
2 thyme sprigs

Stuffing:
15 g (½ oz) butter
1 shallot, chopped
15 g (½ oz) smoked streaky bacon, derinded and chopped
25 g (1 oz) chestnut mushrooms, chopped
25 g (1 oz) open mushrooms, chopped
15 ml (1 tbsp) Drambuie
dried thyme, to taste
freshly grated nutmeg, to taste
salt and freshly ground black pepper

Sauce:
25 g (1 oz) butter
50 g (2 oz) open mushrooms, chopped
30 ml (2 tbsp) Drambuie
7.5 ml (1½ tsp) heather honey
300 ml (½ pint) rich brown game stock

To Garnish:
watercress sprigs

1 Mix the marinade ingredients together in a shallow dish, add the venison and leave in a cool place to marinate for at least 30 minutes.

2 To prepare the stuffing, melt the butter in a pan, add the shallot and fry for 1-2 minutes, to soften. Add the bacon and mushrooms and stir well. Add the Drambuie, and thyme, nutmeg and salt and pepper to taste. Cook gently for 10 minutes, until the liquid has evaporated.

3 Remove the venison from the marinade and dry well on kitchen paper. Cut a deep slit along one side to make a pocket and stuff with the mushroom mixture. Tie at intervals with string.

4 Heat the oil in a pan, add the venison and fry quickly for 1 minute, turning, to seal. Remove the string. Wrap the venison in the bacon rashers and re-tie. Place on a rack over a roasting pan half-filled with hot water and cook in a preheated oven at 200°C (400°F) mark 6 for 25-30 minutes.

5 Meanwhile, make the sauce. Melt half of the butter in a pan, add the mushrooms and cook for 2-3 minutes, to soften. Stir in the Drambuie and honey, then add the stock. Bring to the boil and boil until reduced by half. Beat in the remaining butter, in small pieces, whisking constantly until smooth and thickened. Strain, return to the pan and keep warm.

6 Remove venison from oven and increase temperature to 220°C (425°F) mark 7. Remove the bacon rashers from the venison. Return the fillet to the oven for 5 minutes, to brown the outside.

7 To serve, cut the fillet into 6 slices. Place 3 slices on each warmed serving plate, pour the sauce around and garnish with watercress. Serve with Celeriac Game Chips and Leeks in Thyme Butter (see page 55).

CELERIAC GAME CHIPS

1 small celeriac root
sunflower or groundnut oil, for deep-
  frying
sea salt

1 Peel the celeriac thickly and slice in a food processor to 2 mm (¹⁄₈ inch) slices.

2 Heat the oil in a deep pan to 180°C (350°F), add the celeriac slices and deep-fry until golden brown. Drain on kitchen paper and season with sea salt.

LEEKS IN THYME BUTTER

6 small leeks
25 g (1 oz) butter
6 thyme sprigs, tied in a bunch

1 Trim the leeks to 7.5-10 cm (3-4 inch) lengths, then slice in half lengthways. Wash thoroughly.

2 Melt the butter in a pan, add the leeks and thyme, cover and cook gently for about 10 minutes, until tender. Remove the thyme before serving.

CRANBERRY AND CLEMENTINE SORBET

Sorbet:
150 g (½ oz) cranberries
1 cinnamon stick
small piece of fresh root ginger
strip of orange rind
juice of 3 clementines
50 g (2 oz) caster sugar
5 ml (1 tsp) powdered gelatine
5 ml (1 tsp) Mandarin or other orange-
    flavoured liqueur
¼ egg white

To Serve:
30 ml (2 tbsp) Greek yogurt
30 ml (2 tbsp) single cream
5 ml (1 tsp) caster sugar
4 cranberries

1 To make the sorbet, put the cranberries, cinnamon stick, ginger, orange rind and the juice of 1 clementine in a pan and cook for 5-10 minutes, until the cranberries burst their skins.

2 Place the remaining clementine juice in a pan, add the sugar and stir until dissolved, then bring to the boil and boil for 1-2 minutes, to form a syrup. Remove from the heat and leave to cool.

3 Dissolve the gelatine in 30 ml (2 tbsp) hot water.

4 Rub the cranberries through a sieve into a jug. Add the syrup, gelatine and liqueur. Set aside 15 ml (1 tbsp) for decoration. Leave the remainder until quite cool, then churn in an ice-cream maker for 5-10 minutes, until beginning to freeze.

5 Whisk the egg white until stiff, add to the sorbet and churn for another 5 minutes. Press into 2 heart-shaped moulds lined with cling film and freeze.

6 Whisk together the yogurt, cream and sugar and chill until required.

7 To serve, turn out the sorbet hearts onto 2 serving plates and pour a spoonful of the yogurt cream around them. Dot the sauce with the reserved cranberry juice and feather it out with a cocktail stick. Decorate with cranberries and serve with the Autumn Leaf Biscuits (see page 57).

AUTUMN LEAF BISCUITS

½ egg white, whisked
25 g (1 oz) caster sugar
15 g (½ oz) plain flour
15 g (½ oz) butter, melted
2.5 ml (½ tsp) clementine juice
1.25 ml (¼ tsp) cocoa powder
5 ml (1 tsp) grated clementine rind

1 Place the egg white and sugar in a bowl and whisk together until light and frothy. Fold in the flour, butter and clementine juice. Set aside 15 ml (1 tbsp) of the mixture, adding the cocoa powder to it. Add the clementine rind to the remainder.

2 Place 4 spoonfuls of the orange mixture well apart on a baking sheet lined with non-stick baking parchment, forming into leaf shapes.

3 Pipe a line of the reserved cocoa mixture along the centre of each 'leaf' and feather it outwards with a cocktail stick to form 'veins'. Bake in a preheated oven at 190°C (375°F) mark 5 for 4 minutes.

4 Leave to cool slightly, then remove while still pliable and pinch the base of the 'leaves'. Carefully place on a wire rack to cool.

REGULAR HEATS
— The South East & Channel Isles—

Contestants
Cathy Merrick • Joanna Bruce • Rachel de Caen

Panel of Judges
Sue Lawrence • Rick Wakeman • Loyd Grossman

Joanna Bruce's Menu

MAIN COURSE
Fillet of Scottish Salmon with Leek and Marsala Sauce
Buttered New Potatoes
Selection of Baby Vegetables
"It was superb" **Sue Lawrence**

DESSERT
Small Choux Buns with a Cointreau Sabayon and Fresh Fruits
"The sabayon was incredibly well made" **Loyd**

Twelve year old Joanna Bruce lives on the south coast at Goring-by-Sea, where she loves to cycle along the seafront. Joanna and her mother are enthusiastic treasure hunters and enjoy combing the local beaches, with the aid of their metal detector! Joanna also spends a lot of time at her grandparents home, helping to care for their impressive collection of birds, which includes canaries, parakeets, quails and weavers.

FILLET OF SCOTTISH SALMON WITH LEEKS AND MARSALA SAUCE

*2 Scottish salmon fillets, each 175 g
(6 oz)*
15 ml (1 tbsp) olive oil (approximately)
salt and freshly ground black pepper
squeeze of lemon juice
50 g (2 oz) unsalted butter
1 leek, finely chopped
60 ml (2 fl oz) Marsala
30 ml (2 tbsp) crème fraîche
15 ml (1 tbsp) finely chopped parsley

1 Brush the salmon with olive oil, then season with a little salt and pepper and a squeeze of lemon juice. Place in an oiled ovenproof dish, cover with foil and cook in a preheated oven at 200°C (400°F) mark 6 for 12 minutes.

2 Meanwhile, melt the butter in a pan, adding 5 ml (1 tsp) olive oil to prevent burning. Add the leek and cook gently for about 5 minutes, until just tender.

3 Remove the salmon from the oven and leave to rest, covered, in a warm place for 10 minutes.

4 Season the leek with salt and pepper to taste, then add the Marsala and boil rapidly to burn off the alcohol. Add the crème fraîche and reduce until the sauce reaches a pouring consistency. Add the parsley and check the seasoning. Keep warm.

5 To serve, heat a metal skewer over a flame or very hot plate, until really hot. Unwrap the salmon and sear quickly with the skewer. Serve with the sauce, accompanied by boiled new potatoes, baby sweetcorn and asparagus.

SMALL CHOUX BUNS WITH COINTREAU SABAYON AND FRESH FRUITS

Choux Buns:
25 g (1 oz) butter
75 ml (3 fl oz) water
pinch of salt
32 g (1¼ oz) plain flour, sifted
1 egg, beaten

Cointreau Sabayon:
2 egg yolks
50 ml (2 fl oz) Cointreau
15 ml (1 tbsp) caster sugar

To Finish:
60 ml (2 fl oz) double cream
a little icing sugar, sifted
selection of 3 fresh fruits, prepared as
   necessary (see below)

1 To make the choux buns, put the butter, water and salt in a pan. Heat gently until melted, then bring to the boil. Remove the pan from the heat and immediately tip in all of the flour. Beat vigorously with a wooden spoon until the mixture is smooth and leaves the side of the pan clean. Gradually beat in the egg, until a smooth glossy paste is formed.

2 Spoon the mixture into 6 small mounds, spaced well apart, on a dampened baking sheet. Bake in a preheated oven at 400°C (200°F) mark 6 for about 25 minutes, until well risen and golden. Transfer to a wire rack and split each bun to release the steam. Leave to cool.

3 Meanwhile, make the sabayon. Place all the ingredients in a heatproof bowl and beat well to mix. Place the bowl over a pan of very hot, but not boiling, water and whisk until the mixture thickens sufficiently to hold 'peaks' when the whisk is lifted.

4 Whip the cream until thick and sweeten with a little icing sugar, to taste. Cut a 'lid' off each of the choux buns and set aside.

5 Place a spoonful of sabayon on each serving plate and arrange 3 choux buns on top. Fill with the cream and fruit, using a different fruit for each bun. Top with the sabayon, replace the lids and dust with icing sugar. Decorate the plates with any remaining fruit.

COOK'S TIP

Choose fruits that combine well in flavour and look good together, such as raspberries, orange and kiwi fruit; or strawberries, pineapple and banana. Slice, dice or segment as necessary into bite-sized pieces that will easily fill the buns. Fill each choux bun with a different fruit. Use any remaining fruit to decorate the plates, brushing with lemon juice if necessary to stop discolouration.

— The South East & Channel Isles—

Contestants

Cathy Merrick • Joanna Bruce • Rachel de Caen

Panel of Judges

Sue Lawrence • Rick Wakeman • Loyd Grossman

Rachel de Caen's Menu

MAIN COURSE

Parcels of Chicken and Bacon with an Orange and Lemon Stuffing, served with a Butter and Parsley Sauce

Tomato Cases with a Swede and Carrot Filling

"...very well executed" **Loyd**

DESSERT

Raspberry and Kirsch Surprise

"The pudding was lovely. I thought it was fabulous" **Sue Lawrence**

Rachel de Caen is fifteen years old and comes from St Lawrence in Jersey. Rachel is a devoted horsewoman and she and her friends enjoy nothing more than an afternoon ride along one of the island's beautiful beaches. Rachel is also an enthusiastic member of the St John Ambulance. At home Rachel enjoys helping her father with his carpentry.

PARCELS OF CHICKEN AND BACON WITH AN ORANGE AND LEMON STUFFING, SERVED WITH A BUTTER AND PARSLEY SAUCE

1 orange
1 lemon
15 ml (1 tbsp) finely chopped parsley
1½ slices of bread, made into crumbs
1 small onion, finely chopped
salt and freshly ground black pepper
2 boneless chicken breasts, each about
    150 g (5 oz)
4 rashers unsmoked back bacon,
    derinded

Butter and Parsley Sauce:
1 egg yolk
15 ml (1 tbsp) tarragon wine vinegar
150 g (5 oz) unsalted butter
45 ml (3 tbsp) finely chopped parsley

To Garnish:
2 dill sprigs

1 Peel the orange, removing all pith, and chop the flesh coarsely. Cut 2 slices from the lemon, and set aside for garnish. Grate the rind from the remaining lemon and squeeze the juice. Mix the lemon juice and rind, orange flesh, parsley, breadcrumbs and onion together. Season to taste with salt and pepper.

2 Flatten the chicken breasts with a rolling pin or meat mallet, until they are very thin. Place half of the stuffing in the centre of each chicken piece, then roll up the chicken, completely enclosing the stuffing. Wrap the parcels in the bacon and secure with cocktail sticks. Place on a baking tray and cook in a preheated oven at 190°C (375°F) mark 5 for 25 minutes.

3 Meanwhile, prepare the sauce. Place the egg yolk and vinegar in a heatproof bowl and beat together until light in colour and texture. Place the bowl over a pan of gently simmering water, on a low heat, and whisk until the mixture is thick and creamy.

4 Gradually add the butter, in small pieces, whisking continuously, until all the butter has been added or the sauce has reached the required thickness. Don't add the butter too fast or let the sauce boil or it will curdle. Stir in the parsley and salt and pepper to taste.

5 To serve, pour the sauce onto 2 serving plates, arrange the chicken parcels in the centre and garnish with dill and the reserved lemon slices. Serve with Tomato Cases with a Swede and Carrot Filling (see page 63).

TOMATO CASES WITH A SWEDE AND CARROT FILLING

75 g (3 oz) carrot, finely chopped
75 g (3 oz) swede, finely chopped
knob of butter
25 g (1 oz) mature Cheddar cheese,
  grated
salt and freshly ground black pepper
4 tomatoes

To Garnish:
4 parsley sprigs

1 Cook the carrot and swede in boiling water for 10 minutes or until cooked. Drain well, then mash with a knob of butter. Whilst still hot, add the cheese, stirring it in until melted. Season with salt and pepper to taste.

2 Slice the tops off the tomatoes and scoop out the insides, being careful not to pierce the skins.

3 Fill the tomato cases with the vegetable mixture and cook in a preheated oven at 190°C (375°F) mark 5 for 10-15 minutes. Garnish with parsley to serve.

COOK'S TIP

Choose tomatoes with flat bottoms or they will collapse during cooking. Use the scooped-out tomato pulp in a sauce or soup.

RASPBERRY AND KIRSCH SURPRISE

Cases:
25 g (1 oz) raspberries
7.5 ml (1½ tsp) brown sugar
30 ml (2 tbsp) kirsch
10 sponge fingers

Mousse:
200 g (7 oz) raspberries
1 gelatine leaf or 30 ml (2 tbsp)
   powdered gelatine
15 ml (1 tbsp) icing sugar, sifted
15 ml (1 tbsp) lemon juice
¾ egg white
60 ml (2 fl oz) double cream, whipped
125 g (4 oz) milk chocolate, melted
125 g (4 oz) amaretti biscuits, crushed

To Decorate:
2 mint sprigs
15 ml (1 tbsp) cocoa powder

1 The day before serving, make the cases. Press the raspberries through a nylon sieve to remove the pips. Put the raspberry purée, sugar and kirsch in a small pan and heat gently until the sugar has dissolved.

2 Cut the sponge fingers to fit 2 small round individual moulds, each about 7.5 cm (3 inches) in diameter. Soak the fingers briefly in the raspberry sauce, then arrange around the inside of the moulds. Place in the refrigerator overnight.

3 To make the mousse, set aside 2 raspberries for decoration. Work the remainder to a purée in a food processor. Place the raspberry purée in a pan and heat gently. Add the gelatine leaf or sprinkle in the powdered gelatine and stir until dissolved. Add the icing sugar and lemon juice and mix well.

4 Whisk the egg white in a bowl until stiff, then fold into the raspberry purée. Fold in the cream. Pour into the prepared cases and chill for about 35 minutes, until set.

5 Turn out the mousses onto 2 serving plates. Pour over the melted chocolate to cover, then coat immediately with the amaretti crumbs. Decorate with the reserved raspberries and mint sprigs, then dust with cocoa powder to serve.

COOK'S TIP
Do not leave the soaked sponge fingers in the refrigerator for more than 48 hours or they will go soggy.

Contestants
Ross Spence • Kathryn Currie • Thomas Fletcher

Panel of Judges
Martin Blunos • Julie Peasgood • Loyd Grossman

WINNER

Ross Spence's Menu

MAIN COURSE

Char-grilled Pavé of Gravadlax Salmon on a Bed of Leeks with a Light Mustard and Dill-flavoured Sauce

"...a very good combination of ingredients... the textures and tastes all went together" **Martin Blunos**

DESSERT

Crème Brulée Mousse with Macerated Fruits, served with a Mango and Passion Fruit Sauce

"Expert in the sauce department" **Julie Peasgood**

Ross Spence from Banchory in Kincardinshire is fourteen years of age. Ross is a keen fisherman and spends many a lazy afternoon fishing in the river Dee, which flows past the bottom of his garden. He's also an enthusiastic collector of wine labels, and enjoys playing croquet.

CHAR-GRILLED PAVÉ OF GRAVADLAX

1 side of salmon
freshly ground black pepper

Marinade:
300 g (10 oz) sea salt
300 g (10 oz) sugar
grated rind of 2 oranges
2 lemons
10 ml (2 tsp) juniper berries
10 ml (2 tsp) mustard seeds
150 g (5 oz) chopped fresh dill
5 ml (1 tsp) olive oil

Sauce:
150 g (5 oz) butter
2 shallots, finely chopped
150 ml (¼ pint) white wine
5 ml (1 tsp) finely chopped dill, stalks
    reserved
300 ml (½ pint) fish stock
200 ml (7 fl oz) double cream
wholegrain mustard, to taste
1 tomato, skinned, seeded and
    chopped

For the Leeks:
25 g (1 oz) butter
150 g (6 oz) leeks, cut into julienne

To Garnish:
dill sprigs

1 Place all the ingredients for the marinade in a bowl. Add the salmon and leave to marinate in a cool place for 1 day.

2 Remove the salmon from the marinade and cut two 175 g (6 oz) fillets. Heat a metal skewer over a flame or very hot plate until very hot and use to sear the salmon in a criss-cross pattern. Season with pepper, place on a greased baking tray and cook in a preheated oven at 160°C (325°F) mark 3 for 5-8 minutes, until tender.

3 Meanwhile, prepare the sauce. Cut 125 g (4 oz) of the butter into cubes and place in a bowl of iced water. Melt the remaining butter in a pan, add the shallots, cover and sweat for 2 minutes. Add the wine and the stalks from the dill and boil to reduce by half. Add the fish stock and reduce by a further third. Lower the heat, stir in the cream and simmer for 5 minutes. Pass through a chinois or fine-meshed sieve, return to the cleaned pan and keep warm while preparing the leeks.

4 Melt the butter in a pan, add the leeks and pepper to taste and sauté for 2-3 minutes until softened.

5 Whisk the chilled diced butter into the sauce, a piece at a time, making sure each piece is thoroughly incorporated before adding the next. When finished, the sauce should be smooth and shiny. Stir in the mustard. Add the chopped dill and tomato concasse.

6 To serve, arrange the leeks in the centre of 2 warmed serving plates, pour the sauce around and arrange the salmon on top of the leeks. Garnish with dill.

COOK'S TIP

To prepare the gravadlax you will need to marinate a whole side of salmon. For this recipe you will need to cut 2 cutlets from this; store the rest of the salmon in the refrigerator and use as required.

CRÈME BRULÉE MOUSSE WITH MACERATED FRUITS

Mousse:
300 ml (½ pint) single cream
300 ml (½ pint) milk
1 vanilla pod
5 egg yolks
150 g (5 oz) caster sugar
4 gelatine leaves
300 ml (½ pint) double cream, whipped

Caramel:
175 g (6 oz) granulated sugar
juice of 1 lime

Macerated Fruits:
50 g (2 oz) mango, diced
50 g (2 oz) strawberries, diced
1 kiwi fruit, diced
50 g (2 oz) passion fruit
5 ml (1 tsp) Grand Marnier or orange-
 flavoured liqueur

Mango and Passion Fruit Sauce:
2 passion fruit
½ mango, diced
juice of ½ lime

To Finish:
2 mint sprigs

1 First, make the caramel. Put the sugar and lime juice in a pan. Heat gently, stirring, until dissolved, then increase the heat and cook to a dark caramel, without stirring. Carefully pour into 2 ramekins, tilt to coat the bases and set aside.

2 To make the mousse, place the single cream, milk and vanilla pod in a pan and bring to the boil.

3 Whisk the egg yolks and sugar together in a bowl. Pour on the hot cream mixture, whisking all the time. Return to the saucepan and cook, stirring constantly, until thickened. Do not allow to boil or the mixture will curdle. Pass through a sieve into a clean bowl. Add the gelatine and stir until dissolved. Stand the bowl over a larger bowl of ice and leave to cool until on the point of setting, then fold in the whipped cream. Spoon the mousse over the caramel in the ramekins and chill in the refrigerator until set.

4 Meanwhile, prepare the macerated fruits. Mix the fruits with the Grand Marnier in a bowl and chill in the refrigerator.

5 To prepare the sauce, halve the passion fruit and scoop out the pulp and seeds into a blender or food processor. Add the mango and lime juice and work until smooth. Pass through a nylon sieve into a bowl.

6 To serve turn out each mousse onto a serving plate and drizzle over any remaining caramel. Arrange the macerated fruits around the mousse, then surround with the sauce. Decorate with mint.

REGIONAL HEATS
Scotland

Contestants
Ross Spence • Kathryn Currie • Thomas Fletcher

Panel of Judges
Martin Blunos • Julie Peasgood • Loyd Grossman

Kathryn Currie's Menu

MAIN COURSE
Timbale of Trout and Sole stuffed with a Prawn and Mushroom Mousse, served with a Champagne and Dill Sauce

New Potatoes flavoured with Herbs

Glazed Asparagus

"Her presentation was great" **Martin Blunos**

DESSERT
Orange Pasta filled with Peach and Amaretti, served with an Orange Sauce

"The dessert was brilliant" **Martin Blunos**

Kathryn Currie from Kippen in Stirlingshire is thirteen years old. She enjoys taking long walks with her family – the ideal way to appreciate the beautiful countryside surrounding her home. Kathryn is also a promising pianist. An enthusiastic Guide, Kathryn recently played one of the leading roles in the First Kippen Guide's pantomime.

TIMBALE OF TROUT AND SOLE STUFFED WITH A PRAWN AND MUSHROOM MOUSSE

1 trout fillet
1 sole fillet

Filling:
5 g (¼ oz) butter
30 g (1¼ oz) mushrooms, finely chopped
40 g (1½ oz) shelled prawns, finely chopped
7 g (¼ oz) plain flour
squeeze of lemon juice, to taste
1 egg, separated
2.5 ml (½ tsp) finely chopped basil
salt and freshly ground black pepper

Sauce:
150 ml (¼ pint) Champagne
150 ml (¼ pint) single cream
5 g (¼ oz) butter
10 g (2 tsp) chopped dill

To Garnish:
2 prawns
4 basil leaves

1 To prepare the filling, melt the butter in a pan, add the mushrooms and sauté for a few minutes until softened. Add the prawns and flour, then stir in the lemon juice and egg yolk. Add the basil, and salt and pepper to taste. Remove from the heat. Whisk the egg white until stiff, then fold into the mushroom mixture.

2 Grease and base-line two large ramekin dishes. Cut the trout and sole fillets in half lengthways and use to line the ramekins. Fill with the mushroom mixture and cover the ramekins with greased greaseproof paper.

3 Stand the ramekins in an ovenproof dish containing enough water to come halfway up the sides. Cook in a preheated oven at 180°C (350°F) mark 4 for 20 minutes.

4 Meanwhile, make the sauce. Pour the Champagne and cream into a pan, add the butter and bring to the boil. Boil gently until reduced to a pouring consistency. Add the dill.

5 To serve, turn out the fish ramekins onto warmed serving plates. Surround with the sauce and garnish with the prawns and basil. Serve with glazed asparagus and herbed potatoes.

ORANGE PASTA FILLED WITH PEACH AND AMARETTI

Orange Pasta:
125 g (4 oz) plain flour
grated rind of ½ orange
½ egg
2.5 ml (½ tsp) olive oil
60 ml (2 fl oz) orange juice

Filling:
½ peach
50 g (2 oz) amaretti biscuits
6 raspberries

Orange Sauce:
90 ml (3 fl oz) orange juice
10 ml (2 tsp) caster sugar
2.5 ml (½ tsp) cornflour
5 ml (1 tsp) Grand Marnier or other
*   orange-flavoured liqueur*

To Decorate:
few orange segments

1 To make the pasta, sift the flour into a mixing bowl and add the orange rind. Make a well in the centre. Beat the egg with the olive oil and orange juice. Add to the well and gradually mix into the flour, until the mixture holds together in a ball, and isn't sticky. Wrap in a clean tea-towel and leave to rest while preparing the filling.

2 Immerse the peach in a bowl of boiling water for 30 seconds to loosen the skin. Crush the amaretti biscuits with 4 raspberries. Peel and mash the peach flesh, then mix with the crushed amaretti biscuits.

3 Roll out the pasta thinly using a pasta machine. Pass the dough through the machine repeatedly, gradually narrowing the setting by one notch each time until you reach the last but one setting. Cut out 2 large circles of pasta. Divide the filling between the circles, placing it in the centre, fold the dough over and seal the edges well.

4 Cook the pasta in a large pan of boiling water for 1-2 minutes, until *al dente*, cooked but firm to the bite. Drain thoroughly.

5 To make the sauce, blend all the ingredients together in a pan and bring to the boil, stirring. Cook, stirring, until thickened and smooth.

6 To serve, pool the sauce on 2 serving plates and arrange the pasta on top. Decorate with a few orange segments and the reserved raspberries.

Scotland

Contestants
Ross Spence • Kathryn Currie • Thomas Fletcher

Panel of Judges
Martin Blunos • Julie Peasgood • Loyd Grossman

Thomas Fletcher's Menu

MAIN COURSE
Scottish Poached Salmon with a Cucumber and Dill Sauce

Steamed Vegetables

Wild and Basmati Rice

"He cooked the salmon very well indeed... very moist, very succulent... and I liked the sauce" **Julie Peasgood**

DESSERT
Oatmeal Treacle Tart with Lemon and Walnuts

"It looked very appetising" **Julie Peasgood**

Thomas Fletcher is thirteen years old and comes from Uddington, near Glasgow. Thomas is very involved in the activities relating to the twinning of his town with the French town of Châtellerault. This includes contributing to and printing the monthly newsletter. A patrol leader in the scouts, Thomas also loves absailing.

SCOTTISH POACHED SALMON WITH A CUCUMBER AND DILL SAUCE

2 salmon steaks, each about 150 g
  (5 oz)
6 peppercorns
1 bay leaf
30 ml (2 fl oz) red wine vinegar
1 dill sprig

Sauce:
½ cucumber
25 ml (1 fl oz) dry white wine
15 g (½ oz) butter
15 g (½ oz) plain flour
90 ml (3 fl oz) single cream
5 ml (1 tsp) lemon juice
salt and freshly ground black pepper
1 dill sprig

1 First make the sauce. Peel the cucumber, leaving on some of the skin, then cut in half. Roughly chop one half and place in a food processor or blender. Add the wine and work until smooth.

2 Dice the other cucumber half. Heat the butter in a pan, add the diced cucumber, cover and sweat for about 10 minutes.

3 Stir in the flour, add the puréed cucumber, then gradually stir in the cream. Cook gently for about 5 minutes. Add the lemon juice, and salt and pepper to taste.

4 Snip the leaves from the dill sprig, using a pair of scissors and stir into the sauce. Keep warm over very low heat while cooking the salmon.

5 Place the salmon steaks in a shallow pan and add sufficient water to barely cover. Add the peppercorns, bay leaf, red wine vinegar and dill. Bring to the boil and allow the cooking liquid to boil vigorously for 6 minutes. Take off the heat and leave, covered, to rest until ready to serve.

6 Carefully lift the salmon steaks onto warmed serving plates. Serve with the sauce and accompaniments.

STEAMED VEGETABLES

½ courgette
12 mangetouts
1 carrot
6 baby corn cobs

1 Using a canelle knife, cut grooves along the length of the courgette skin to create a ribbed pattern. Cut the courgette into thick rounds, then halve these rounds.

2 Top and tail the mangetouts. Cut the carrot into small fingers. Put all the vegetables in a vegetable steamer.

3 Bring a large pan of water to the boil, place the steamer on top and steam until the vegetables are tender.

WILD AND BASMATI RICE

125 g (4 oz) mixed wild and basmati
  rice

1 Put the rice in a pan and add sufficient water to cover by about 2.5 cm (1 inch). Bring to the boil, then reduce the heat to a simmer and cook for about 45 minutes, until the rice is tender but still with a 'bite' and the water is absorbed.

2 Fork through lightly to serve.

OATMEAL TREACLE TART WITH LEMON AND WALNUTS

Pastry:
75 g (3 oz) self-raising flour
75 g (3 oz) wholemeal flour
40 g (1½ oz) butter, in pieces
40 g (1½ oz) lard, in pieces

Filling:
50 g (2 oz) medium oatmeal
3 slices wholemeal bread, crusts
   removed and made into crumbs
5 g (¼ tsp) ground ginger
40 g (1½ oz) shelled walnuts
grated rind and juice of 1 lemon
37.5 ml (2½ tbsp) golden syrup
beaten egg, to glaze

To Serve:
3 apple slices
3 walnut halves
extra-thick double cream, whipped

1 To make the pastry, sift the self-raising and wholemeal flours into a mixing bowl, add the butter and lard and rub in until the mixture resembles breadcrumbs. Add 30-45 ml (2-3 tbsp) water and mix to a smooth dough. Wrap in cling film and chill while preparing the filling.

2 Toast the oatmeal under a moderate grill until golden brown, turning with a spoon if necessary. Transfer to a pan and add the breadcrumbs, ginger, walnuts, lemon juice and rind, and the golden syrup. Heat gently, stirring well to mix. Remove from the heat and set aside.

3 Roll out the pastry thinly on a lightly floured surface and use to line two 10 cm (4 inch) individual flan tins; reserve the trimmings. Spoon in the filling. Roll out the pastry trimmings, cut into long narrow strips and make a lattice pattern over the filling. Brush the pastry lattice with beaten egg.

4 Cook in a preheated oven at 190°C (375°F) mark 5 for 10 minutes, or until the pastry is golden brown. Serve decorated with the apple slices and walnuts, and accompanied by the whipped cream.

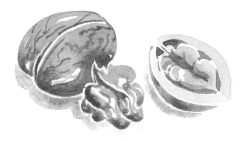

REGIONAL HEATS
The Home Counties

Contestants
Ashley Temple • Anna Hall • Clare Kelley

Panel of Judges
Andrew Radford • Diane Abbott • Loyd Grossman

WINNER

Ashley Temple's Menu

MAIN COURSE
Sizzling Lamb

Mediterranean Couscous

Barrelled Courgettes

"I loved the sizzling lamb" **Loyd**

DESSERT
Cardamom and Yogurt Ice Cream with a Fruit Compote

Pistachio Nut Shortbread

"The ice cream was just heaven… and it went so well with the fruit compote"
Diane Abbott

Thirteen year old Ashley Temple comes from Walton-on-Thames in Surrey. Ashley attends Haliford School and is a member of the athletics squad – high jump being his main event. He's also a keen air scout and takes on a range of responsibilities as a patrol leader.

SIZZLING LAMB

*1 fillet of lamb (loin), about 225 g
(8 oz)*

Marinade:
*300 ml (½ pint) red wine
grated rind of 1 orange
1.25 ml (¼ tsp) tomato purée
1 clove garlic, crushed
1 cm (½ inch) piece fresh root ginger,
  very finely chopped
15 ml (1 tbsp) redcurrant jelly with port
5 ml (1 tsp) olive oil
salt and freshly ground black pepper*

To Garnish:
rosemary sprigs

1 Put all the marinade ingredients in a pan. Bring to the boil and boil steadily until reduced by one third. Leave to cool. Put the lamb in a dish, pour over the cooled marinade and leave to marinate in a cool place overnight.

2 Heat a griddle or heavy-based frying pan until very hot, then drizzle with a little olive oil. Add the lamb and cook quickly, turning, to seal. Drizzle over some of the marinade and cook, turning frequently, until tender but still pink inside.

3 Transfer to a warmed serving plate. Heat the remaining marinade, then strain and pour over the meat. Garnish with rosemary. Cut into thick slices and serve with Mediterranean Couscous and Barelled Courgettes (see page 77).

MEDITERRANEAN COUSCOUS

125-175 g (4-6 oz) couscous
175 ml (6 fl oz) chicken stock, boiling
15 g (½ oz) butter
15 ml (1 tbsp) olive oil
2 spring onions, finely chopped
2 plum tomatoes, skinned, seeded and
  chopped
dash of chilli sauce, to taste
squeeze of lemon juice
salt and freshly ground black pepper

To Garnish:
herb sprigs

1 Place the couscous in a saucepan, pour on the boiling stock and cook for 2 minutes. Remove from the heat and leave to stand for 1 minute. Return to the heat for 2 minutes, checking constantly and adding more stock or water if required. Remove from the heat and leave to stand.

2 Heat the butter and oil in a pan, add the spring onions and tomatoes and sauté for about 5 minutes, until just tender. Add the chilli sauce, lemon juice and salt and pepper to taste. Add to the couscous and cook for 1 minute.

3 Divide between 2 dariole moulds or individual pudding basins, pressing down firmly. Leave for 1½ minutes to set, then unmould onto serving plates. Garnish with herbs to serve.

BARRELLED COURGETTES

2 large courgettes
1 carrot, cut into julienne
small handful of French beans, trimmed
chicken stock, for cooking

1 Hollow out the courgettes, using an apple corer. Stuff them with alternate pieces of carrot and bean until they are 'crammed'.

2 Heat a 2.5 cm (1 inch) depth of chicken stock in a saucepan, add the courgettes and cook for about 10-15 minutes, until just tender. Cut into slices to serve.

CARDAMOM AND YOGURT ICE CREAM

3 cardamom pods
75 g (3 oz) caster sugar
200-250 ml (7-8 fl oz) single cream
60 ml (2 fl oz) double cream
200-250 ml (7-8 fl oz) natural yogurt

Fruit Compote:
50 g (2 oz) blackberries
2 peaches or nectarines, stoned and
*   sliced*
25 g (1 oz) blackcurrants
25 g (1 oz) blueberries
25 g (1 oz) redcurrants
4 plums, stoned and sliced
15 ml (1 tbsp) sugar, or to taste
squeeze of lemon juice

1 Remove the seeds from the cardamom pods and grind to a fine powder, using a pestle and mortar. Place in a bowl with the sugar, single and double creams and the yogurt; stir well. Transfer to an ice-cream maker and churn until firm. Transfer to a freezerproof container and place in the freezer until required.

2 To make the fruit compote, place all the ingredients in a heavy-based pan and simmer very gently for about 20 minutes, until the fruit is tender but still retaining its shape.

3 To serve, scoop the ice cream onto chilled plates. Accompany with the fruit compote and Pistachio Shortbread (see page 79).

COOK'S NOTE

If you do not have an ice-cream maker, freeze in a suitable container, whisking occasionally to break down the ice crystals and ensure a smooth-textured result.

PISTACHIO SHORTBREAD

50 g (2 oz) butter
20 g (¾ oz) icing sugar, sifted
50 g (2 oz) plain flour, sifted
20 g (¾ oz) rice flour, sifted
25 g (1 oz) pistachio nuts, roasted and
very finely chopped

1 Cream the butter and icing sugar together until light and fluffy. Add the flours and beat well, then work in the nuts to yield a stiff paste. Knead lightly, then wrap in cling film and chill for 20-25 minutes.

2 Turn onto a floured board, knead lightly, then roll out to a round, about 1 cm (½ inch) thick. Cut out 5 cm (2 inch) rounds. Place on a greased baking sheet and bake in a preheated oven at 190°C (375°F) mark 5 for 10-15 minutes, until pale golden.

VARIATIONS

Replace the pistachios with roasted almonds or hazelnuts. Add a little finely grated orange rind for a hint of orange.

REGIONAL HEATS
———— The Home Counties ————

Contestants
Ashley Temple • Anna Hall • Clare Kelley

Panel of Judges
Andrew Radford • Diane Abbott • Loyd Grossman

Anna Hall's Menu

MAIN COURSE

Fillet of Salmon with Spinach wrapped in Smoked Salmon with
a Dill Sauce

Sugar Snap Peas à la Française

New Potatoes

"That marriage of the smoked and fresh salmon worked very well"
Andrew Radford

DESSERT

Chocolate Mélange with Strawberry and Passion Fruit Sauce

"The pudding was scrumptious" **Diane Abbott**

———————

A nna Hall from Cheam in Surrey is thirteen years of age.
Anna enjoys swimming and takes to the water for
exercise whenever the opportunity arises. She also loves
looking after young children and frequently lends a hand at
the nearby crèche.

FILLET OF SALMON WITH SPINACH, SMOKED SALMON AND A DILL SAUCE

*2 pieces of salmon fillet, each about
    125 g (4 oz)
125 g (4 oz) spinach leaves
125 g (4 oz) smoked salmon
salt and freshly ground black pepper*

Dill Sauce:
*25 g (1 oz) butter
25 g (1 oz) plain flour
175 ml (6 fl oz) milk
15-30 ml (1-2 tbsp) chopped dill, to
    taste*

To Garnish:
*1 small tomato, skinned, seeded and
    shredded
dill sprigs*

1 Wrap the salmon fillets in spinach leaves, then wrap in the smoked salmon slices to enclose. Place both salmon parcels in the centre of a large square of foil, season with salt and pepper and sprinkle with 15 ml (1 tbsp) water. Wrap tightly in the foil and place on a baking sheet. Cook in a preheated oven at 160°C (325°F) mark 3 for about 25 minutes.

2 Meanwhile, make the sauce. Melt the butter in a pan, stir in the flour and cook, stirring, for 1 minute to make a roux. Remove from the heat and gradually add the milk. Return to the heat and bring to the boil, stirring constantly, until thickened. Stir in the dill and cook for 1 minute.

3 Remove the salmon from the foil with a slotted spoon and arrange on warmed serving plates. Tip the juices from the foil into the sauce and reheat. Pour the juices over the salmon, garnish with the tomato and dill and serve with Sugar Snap Peas à la Française (see page 82) and new potatoes.

SUGAR SNAP PEAS À LA FRANÇAISE

175 g (6 oz) sugar snap peas
½ cos lettuce, cored and shredded
25 g (1 oz) butter
6 spring onions, cut into 2.5 cm (1 inch)
  lengths
salt and freshly ground black pepper

1 Blanch the peas for 20 seconds and the lettuce for 10 seconds in boiling water. Refresh under cold water.

2 Melt the butter in a pan, add the spring onions and fry very gently for 3 minutes. Add the peas and lettuce and stir over medium heat for about 3 minutes, until hot. Season with salt and pepper and serve immediately.

CHOCOLATE MÉLANGE WITH STRAWBERRY AND PASSION FRUIT SAUCE

175 ml (6 fl oz) double cream
175 g (6 oz) plain chocolate, melted
25 g (1 oz) white chocolate, melted

Strawberry and Passion Fruit Sauce:
3 passion fruit
175 g (6 oz) strawberries, puréed
5 ml (1 tsp) caster sugar

To Decorate:
cocoa powder, for dusting
a little natural yogurt

1 Line two 7.5 cm (3 inch) pastry cutters with bakewell paper, to stand 2.5 cm (1 inch) above the rim, and place on 2 serving plates.

2 Whip the cream until it begins to thicken. Quickly fold in the melted plain chocolate. Pour into the lined pastry cutters and smooth the top. Chill for 45 minutes.

3 Using a fine paintbrush, thickly paint the underside of 4 clean rose leaves with the melted white chocolate. Place on a sheet of greaseproof paper and leave in a cool place until set. Carefully peel each leaf away from the chocolate.

4 To make the sauce, halve the passion fruit and scoop out the pulp. Press through a sieve into a bowl, then add the strawberry purée and sugar and stir well to mix.

5 To serve, remove the pastry cutters and paper from the chocolate mélange. Dust with cocoa powder and surround with the sauce. Dot the sauce with yogurt and feather out with a cocktail stick. Decorate with the chocolate leaves.

COOK'S TIP

Pick fresh undamaged rose leaves, with clearly marked veins, and wash and dry thoroughly before coating with chocolate.

Contestants
Ashley Temple • Anna Hall • Clare Kelley

Panel of Judges
Andrew Radford • Diane Abbott • Loyd Grossman

Clare Kelley's Menu

MAIN COURSE

Lamb in a Herb Crust on a Bed of Spinach with a Rosemary
and Redcurrant Sauce

Baby Carrots, Wild Mushrooms and Asparagus

"It was brilliant lamb, and the herb crust worked so well" **Andrew Radford**

DESSERT

Hazelnut and Raspberry Roulade with Raspberry Coulis

"The pudding was a star" **Diane Abbott**

Fourteen year old Clare Kelley comes from Waddesdon in Buckinghamshire. Clare and her family all enjoy tennis and as a member of the county squad, Clare plays in tournaments all over Britain. She's also a keen musician and a talented clarinet player. Clare's other interests include collecting thimbles: she has over a hundred in total, antique and modern, from around the world.

LAMB IN A HERB CRUST ON A BED OF SPINACH WITH ROSEMARY AND REDCURRANT SAUCE

1 fillet of lamb (loin), about 225 g (8 oz)
several sprigs each of flat-leaf parsley, parsley, rosemary, marjoram, thyme and sage, finely chopped (see note)
30 ml (2 tbsp) extra-virgin olive oil

Rosemary and Redcurrant Sauce:
handful of redcurrants
600 ml (1 pint) beef stock
1 fresh rosemary sprig

To Serve:
1 large packet of spinach leaves
salt, to taste
16 asparagus tips
16 baby carrots
15 ml (1 tbsp) oil
10 wild mushrooms

1 Trim away any fat from the outside of the lamb. Put all the herbs in a bowl, add the olive oil and mix together to make a paste. Spread all over the lamb. Place in an ovenproof dish and cook in a preheated oven at 190°C (375°F) mark 5 for about 25 minutes, while preparing the sauce and vegetables.

2 Set aside about 4 redcurrants for garnish. Put the rest in a pan with the stock and rosemary sprig and bring to a steady boil. Cook until reduced and slightly thickened.

3 Put the spinach in a pan with a pinch of salt and add water to a depth of about 1 cm (½ inch). Cook for about 2 minutes, until reduced down, then transfer to one side of a steamer. Cut the asparagus to size and place on the other side of the steamer.

4 Trim the carrots, leaving a little of the green stalks still attached. Place in the steamer pan and add salted water to cover. Bring to the boil, position the steamer on top and cook for 5 minutes, or until the vegetables are tender.

5 Heat the oil in a pan, add the mushrooms and sauté for a few minutes, until tender.

6 Strain the sauce, then reheat.

7 Cut the meat into 8 slices. Divide the spinach between 2 warmed serving plates and arrange the lamb slices on top. Garnish with the redcurrants and serve with the carrots, asparagus and mushrooms.

COOK'S NOTE

Use a little less rosemary than the other herbs for the crust, as the accompanying sauce is also flavoured with rosemary.

HAZELNUT AND RASPBERRY ROULADE WITH RASPBERRY COULIS

50 g (2 oz) hazelnuts, ground
22.5 ml (1½ tbsp) cornflour, sifted
3.75 ml (¾ tsp) baking powder
2 eggs
65 g (2½ oz) caster sugar
600 ml (1 pint) double cream
300 ml (½ pint) single cream
450 g (1 lb) raspberries, halved

Raspberry Coulis:
125 g (4 oz) raspberries
15 ml (1 tbsp) icing sugar, or to taste

To Decorate:
few hazelnuts
grated plain chocolate
few raspberries
mint sprig
icing sugar, for dusting

1 Place the hazelnuts, cornflour and baking powder in a bowl and mix well.

2 Place the eggs and sugar in another bowl and whisk together until light and fluffy. Gently fold in the hazelnut mixture. Turn into an 18 x 28 cm (7 x 11 inch) Swiss roll tin lined with non-stick baking parchment. Bake in a preheated oven at 190°C (375°F) mark 5 for 15-20 minutes or until the mixture has shrunk away from the sides of the tin.

3 Turn out onto a large sheet of greaseproof paper sprinkled with icing sugar. Peel off the lining paper. Leave until completely cold.

4 To make the raspberry coulis, purée the raspberries in a blender or food processor, then pass through a sieve to remove the pips. Sweeten with icing sugar to taste.

5 Whip the creams together until stiff. Spread half over the cold sponge, then cover with the raspberries. Roll up tightly from one long side and place on a serving dish. Cover with the remaining cream and arrange the hazelnuts along the top. Sprinkle the chocolate vertically in stripes down the sides. Decorate with the raspberries and mint, then dust with icing sugar. Serve, cut into slices, on a pool of raspberry coulis. (Serves 4-6)

Contestants

Kate Watkins • Claire Lethbridge • Rebecca Metcalf

Panel of Judges

Mark Hix • Sue Cook • Loyd Grossman

WINNER

Kate Watkins' Menu

MAIN COURSE

Fillet Steak Cacciatora

Potato Rösti

Sugar Snap Peas

Baby Carrots

"Beautifully cooked, nicely presented" **Sue Cook**

DESSERT

Mango Crème Brûlée

"The texture of the brûlée was excellent" **Mark Hix**

Kate Watkins from Longtown in Herefordshire is fifteen years old. Kate is a prefect at Fairfield High School, and manager of the school bank. Living on the family farm, Kate looks after a small collection of her own animals including Billy the heifer and Wiggle and Woggle, her 40 year old donkeys!

FILLET STEAK CACCIATORA

30 ml (2 tbsp) olive oil
2 fillet steaks, each about 175 g (6 oz)
salt and freshly ground black pepper
1 clove garlic, chopped
300 ml (½ pint) red wine
300 ml (½ pint) Marsala
5 ml (1 tsp) fennel seeds
20 ml (4 tsp) tomato purée

To Garnish:
chopped parsley

1 Heat the oil in a frying pan, add the steaks and cook for 2-3 minutes each side, until done to your liking. Season with salt and pepper to taste. Remove from the pan and keep warm.

2 Add the garlic to the pan and fry briefly, then stir in the red wine and Marsala. Cook until reduced to a thick syrup, then stir in the fennel seeds and tomato purée and cook for 1 minute.

3 Pour the sauce over the steaks and garnish with parsley. Serve with sugar snap peas, baby carrots and potato rösti.

POTATO RÖSTI

2 medium potatoes
15 ml (1 tbsp) olive oil
salt and freshly ground black pepper

1 Place the unpeeled potatoes in a saucepan of cold water. Bring to the boil, lower the heat and simmer for 10 minutes. Drain the par-cooked potatoes, leave until cool enough to handle, then remove the skins.

2 Grate the potatoes and season liberally with salt and pepper. Divide in half and shape each portion into a round, about 6 cm (2½ inches) in diameter and 1 cm (½ inch) thick.

3 Heat the oil in a non-stick frying pan, add the rösti and fry for a few minutes each side, until light golden brown. Drain on kitchen paper and serve at once.

MANGO CRÈME BRULÉE

2 egg yolks
15 ml (1 tbsp) icing sugar
10 ml (2 tsp) cornflour
5 ml (1 tsp) vanilla essence
300 ml (½ pint) double cream
1 small ripe mango
22.5 ml (1½ tbsp) granulated sugar

1 Whisk together the egg yolks, icing sugar, cornflour and vanilla essence in a bowl until combined. Put the cream in a saucepan and bring to the boil, then pour onto the egg mixture whisking thoroughly; the mixture should thicken immediately. If it doesn't, return to the pan and cook, stirring, until thickened; do not boil. Let cool slightly.

2 Peel the mango and cut the flesh away from the stone. Slice half of the mango and set aside for the decoration. Cut the rest into chunks.

3 Put a few mango chunks into each of 2 ramekins and pour the cream mixture over the top. Chill in the refrigerator until set.

4 To finish, melt the sugar in a heavy-based saucepan over a high heat, then increase the heat and cook until caramelised. Pour over the set crèmes and chill until ready to serve. Decorate with the reserved mango slices.

Contestants
Kate Watkins • Claire Lethbridge • Rebecca Metcalf

Panel of Judges
Mark Hix • Sue Cook • Loyd Grossman

Claire Lethbridge's Menu

MAIN COURSE

Lamb Fillets wrapped in Spinach and Bacon with a Rosemary Cream Sauce

Glazed Château Potatoes

Broccoli Florets

"The flavours were very good" **Mark Hix**

DESSERT

St Clement's Surprise Pudding

"Really delicious pudding... excellent" **Sue Cook**

Claire Lethbridge from Bingham in Nottinghamshire is fifteen years of age. Claire has spent much of her time this year studying for her GCSE's, including one on Child Development. She also enjoys badminton and plays at the nearby RAF base where her partner, sister Mandy, is based. On Saturdays Claire works at 'Exotics' serving fruit and vegetables to the townsfolk of Bingham.

LAMB FILLETS WRAPPED IN SPINACH AND BACON WITH A ROSEMARY CREAM SAUCE AND GLAZED CHATEAU POTATOES

2 lamb fillets, each about 175 g (6 oz)
seasoned flour, for coating
a little olive oil, for cooking
2 large spinach leaves
8 rashers of streaky bacon, derinded

Rosemary Cream Sauce:
3 shallots, chopped
300 ml (½ pint) lamb stock
few rosemary sprigs
150 ml (¼ pint) double cream

Château Potatoes:
6 potatoes, halved
100 ml (3½ fl oz) lamb stock
  (approximately)
sesame seeds, for sprinkling

1 To cook the potatoes, put them in a roasting tin with enough stock to thinly cover the base of the tin. Cook in a preheated oven at 190°C (375°F) mark 5 for 35 minutes.

2 To prepare the lamb, coat in seasoned flour. Heat a little oil in a heavy-based pan over high heat, add the lamb and fry quickly on both sides to seal. Remove from the pan, reserving any juices. Wrap each fillet in a spinach leaf, then enclose in 4 bacon rashers. Place in a second roasting tin and cook in the oven for 25 minutes.

3 To make the sauce, fry the shallots in the pan used to seal the lamb, until softened. Add the stock, stirring, and bring to the boil. Add the rosemary and cream and cook until reduced to a sauce consistency. Strain through a fine sieve.

4 To serve, arrange the lamb on 2 warmed serving plates and pour over the sauce. Accompany with the potatoes, sprinkled with sesame seeds, and broccoli.

ST CLEMENT'S SURPRISE PUDDING

50 g (2 oz) margarine
125 g (4 oz) caster sugar
15 ml (½ tbsp) grated lemon rind
15 ml (½ tbsp) grated orange rind
2 eggs, separated
300 ml (½ pint) milk
50 g (2 oz) self-raising flour, sifted
60 ml (2 fl oz) lemon juice
60 ml (2 fl oz) orange juice

To Decorate:
6 lemon slices

1 In a mixing bowl, cream the margarine with the sugar and grated fruit rinds until light and fluffy. Beat in the egg yolks and half of the milk, then fold in the flour. Stir in the remaining milk and the lemon and orange juice.

2 Whisk the egg whites until they form soft peaks, then fold into the mixture. Pour into greased ramekin dishes and place in a roasting tin.

3 Pour in boiling water to come half-way up the sides of the dishes. Bake in a preheated oven at 180°C (350°F) mark 4 for 35-45 minutes, until the tops of the puddings are golden brown and firm to the touch. Serve in the ramekins, decorated with lemon slices.

The Midlands

Contestants

Kate Watkins • Claire Lethbridge • Rebecca Metcalf

Panel of Judges

Mark Hix • Sue Cook • Loyd Grossman

Rebecca Metcalf's Menu

MAIN COURSE

French Roast Poussin in a White Wine Sauce

Roast Potatoes

Seasonal Vegetables

"The chicken was beautiful... and the sauce worked very well with it" **Sue Cook**

DESSERT

Petit Pot de Café Chocolat

"The pudding was a tour de force" **Sue Cook**

Thirteen year old Rebecca Metcalf comes from Shifnal in Shropshire. Rebecca is a pupil at Newport Girls High School and her favourite subject is Art. Outside school, Rebecca's interests focus around winter sports. She is particularly keen on ice skating and skiing.

FRENCH ROAST POUSSIN IN A WHITE WINE SAUCE

2 poussins
8 cloves garlic
2 lemons
2 bunches of mixed fresh herbs, eg
    tarragon, parsley, marjoram, thyme,
    oregano, winter savoury, bay leaf
75 ml (5 tbsp) olive oil
salt and freshly ground black pepper
pinch of dried mixed herbs
15 ml (1 tbsp) rowan, redcurrant or
    gooseberry jelly

Sauce:
25 g (1 oz) butter
1 shallot, finely chopped
30 ml (2 tbsp) tarragon vinegar
150 ml (¼ pint) dry white wine
5 ml (1 tsp) arrowroot
125 ml (¼ pint) chicken stock
125 ml (¼ pint) double cream
15-30 ml (1-2 tbsp) chopped tarragon

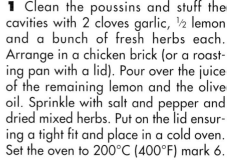

1 Clean the poussins and stuff the cavities with 2 cloves garlic, ½ lemon and a bunch of fresh herbs each. Arrange in a chicken brick (or a roasting pan with a lid). Pour over the juice of the remaining lemon and the olive oil. Sprinkle with salt and pepper and dried mixed herbs. Put on the lid ensuring a tight fit and place in a cold oven. Set the oven to 200°C (400°F) mark 6.

2 After 50 minutes remove the lid and brush the poussins with the jelly. Return to the oven and roast, uncovered, for 20 minutes.

3 Meanwhile, make the sauce. Melt the butter in a heavy-based saucepan, add the shallot and fry until pale golden. Pour in the vinegar and cook over a high heat until the vinegar has evaporated. Add the wine and reduce again until syrupy. Mix the arrowroot with the chicken stock and add to the pan; cook, stirring until thickened. Reduce the heat, season with salt and pepper to taste and simmer gently.

4 Just before serving, turn up the heat and add the cream and chopped tarragon, but do not allow to boil.

5 To serve, remove the poussins from the oven one at a time. Place on a carving dish and cut down one side of the breast bone. Nick the wish-bone in half, and separate the leg and wing at the knuckle joint . Repeat with the other half and arrange on warmed serving plates. Pour on the sauce and serve accompanied by extra jelly, roast potatoes and seasonal vegetables.

PETIT POT DE CAFÉ CHOCOLAT

125 g (4 oz) plain chocolate
5 ml (1 tsp) freeze-dried coffee granules
2 eggs, separated
125 ml (¼ pint) double cream

To Decorate:
cocoa powder, for dusting
few raspberries or grapes (optional)

1 Melt the chocolate in a heatproof bowl over a pan of hot water.

2 Meanwhile, blend the coffee with 10 ml (2 tsp) boiling water, let cool until lukewarm, then add to the melted chocolate. Stir in the egg yolks.

3 Beat the egg whites until stiff. Stir a large spoonful into the chocolate mixture to lighten it, then carefully fold in the rest.

3 Whip the cream until it is quite stiff. Set aside 15 ml (1 tbsp). Add 30 ml (2 tbsp) to the chocolate mixture and blend in, then carefully fold in the rest. Pour into 2 demi-tasse cups or individual serving dishes and chill for 45 minutes.

4 Top with the reserved cream and a sprinkling of cocoa to serve. Decorate the edge of the saucer or plate with a few raspberries or grapes if wished.

Contestants
Jessica Davies • Anna Jarman • Nathalie Wild

Panel of Judges
Phil Vickery • Jean Boht • Loyd Grossman

WINNER

Jessica Davies' Menu

MAIN COURSE
Salmon Mornay with a Seafood Sauce

Green Beans

New Potatoes

"I thought it was absolutely perfect and so well balanced" **Jean Boht**

DESSERT
Dominican Bananas with Caribbean Cream

"...perfectly cooked. It was very good" **Phil Vickery**

Ten year old Jessica Davies comes from Clavering in Essex. Jessica is an enthusiastic golfer and spends many an afternoon enjoying a round of golf with her grandfather, who's a stalwart of the Saffron Walden Golf Club. Jessica also loves drama – both acting and writing – and her drama group have recently been working on a play about Bosnian refugees.

SALMON MORNAY WITH A SEAFOOD SAUCE

175 g (6 oz) mixed wild rice and long
  grain rice
2 eggs
175 g (6 oz) salmon fillet
65 g (2½ oz) butter
15 ml (1 tbsp) plain flour
350 ml (12 fl oz) milk
125 g (4 oz) Cheddar cheese, grated

Topping:
50 g (2 oz) breadcrumbs
50 g (2 oz) Cheddar cheese, grated

Seafood Sauce:
50 g (2 oz) butter
10 ml (2 tsp) plain flour
250 ml (8 fl oz) milk
125 ml (4 fl oz) white wine
2.5 ml (½ tsp) tomato purée
25 g (1 oz) cooked shelled prawns
25 g (1 oz) cooked shelled mussels
2.5 ml (½ tsp) chopped oregano
freshly ground black pepper
dash of Tabasco, to taste

To Garnish:
lemon slices
cucumber slices

1 Place the rice in a saucepan with 550 ml (18 fl oz) cold water. Bring to the boil and simmer, uncovered, until tender. Drain, rinse and set aside.

2 Place the eggs in another saucepan, cover with cold water, bring to the boil and simmer for 7 minutes. Remove the eggs from the water and set aside.

3 Place the salmon in an ovenproof dish, dot with 15 g (½ oz) butter and cook in a preheated oven at 190°C (375°F) mark 5 for 6 minutes.

4 Meanwhile, make the cheese sauce. Melt the remaining butter in a saucepan, add the flour and blend to a smooth paste. Cook, stirring, for 1 minute, then add the milk gradually, stirring all the time. Stir in the cheese and bring to simmering point, then remove from the heat.

5 Turn the cooked rice into an oven-proof dish, spreading it evenly over the base. Flake the cooked salmon and spread over the rice. Shell and roughly chop the hard-boiled eggs and sprinkle on top of the salmon.

6 Pour over the cheese sauce, then sprinkle with the mixed breadcrumbs and grated cheese. Return to the oven at 200°C (400°F) mark 6 for about 10 minutes until the top is golden.

7 To make the seafood sauce, melt the butter in a saucepan, add the flour and blend to a smooth paste. Cook, stirring, for 1 minute, then gradually stir in the milk. Add the wine, tomato purée, prawns, mussels, oregano and pepper to taste. Bring to the boil, stirring, then add a dash of Tabasco.

8 Serve the salmon garnished with the lemon and cucumber. Hand the sauce separately. Accompany with new potatoes and green beans.

DOMINICAN BANANAS WITH CARIBBEAN CREAM

1 large banana
30 ml (2 tbsp) Dominican rum
30 ml (2 tbsp) caster sugar
2 eggs
75 g (3 oz) desiccated coconut
30 ml (2 tbsp) apricot jam

To Serve:
7.5 ml (1½ tsp) Malibu
90 ml (3 fl oz) double cream

1 Slice the banana and arrange in 2 large greased ramekins. Sprinkle with the rum.

2 Place the sugar and eggs in a bowl and beat well. Add the coconut and jam and blend well. Pour over the bananas and bake in a preheated oven at 180°C (350°F) mark 4 for 25 minutes, until golden.

3 Add the Malibu to the cream and stir thoroughly. Serve with the pudding.

Contestants
Jessica Davies • Anna Jarman • Nathalie Wild

Panel of Judges
Phil Vickery • Jean Boht • Loyd Grossman

Anna Jarman's Menu

MAIN COURSE
Pork in a Herby Cream Sauce

Pink-fir Potatoes

Spinach Timbale

Glazed Baby Carrots with Parsley

"The food was very good... well balanced and very simple" **Phil Vickery**

DESSERT
Lemon Soufflé Custard

"The lemon pudding was outstanding" **Phil Vickery**

Anna Jarman from Cambridge is twelve years of age and attends the Netherhall Lower School. As a keen cross-country runner, she keeps very fit. Anna is also a talented musician with a beautiful singing voice; the flute is her favourite instrument. Bird-watching is another favourite pastime and she often goes with her father to the nearby Fowlmere nature reserve.

PORK IN A HERBY CREAM SAUCE

15 g (½ oz) butter
2 pork chops
salt and freshly ground black pepper

Herby Cream Sauce:
15 g (½ oz) butter
2 shallots, chopped
10 ml (2 tsp) capers
3 gherkins, chopped
15 ml (1 tbsp) plain flour
125 ml (4 fl oz) dry white wine
100 ml (3½ fl oz) soured cream
15 ml (1 tbsp) chopped parsley

To Garnish:
chopped parsley

1 Melt the butter in a pan. Season the chops with salt and pepper, add to the pan and cook for 10-15 minutes, turning once, until the juices run clear.

2 Meanwhile, prepare the sauce. Melt the butter in a pan, add the shallots and sauté for 3-4 minutes. Stir in the capers and gherkins and cook for 2-3 minutes. Stir in the flour and cook, stirring, for 1 minute. Add the wine and bring to the boil, stirring constantly. Remove from the heat, then stir in the cream and parsley.

3 To serve, pour the sauce onto 2 serving plates, arrange the pork chops on top and sprinkle with chopped parsley. Serve with boiled potatoes, glazed baby carrots and Spinach Timbale (see page 101).

SPINACH TIMBALE

225 g (8 oz) spinach leaves
25 g (1 oz) butter
freshly grated nutmeg, to taste

1 Cook the spinach in a tightly covered pan with just the water clinging to the leaves after washing, for 3 minutes.

2 Drain the spinach thoroughly, using your hands to squeeze out all the liquid.

3 Melt the butter in the cleaned pan, add the spinach and nutmeg and cook for 1 minute, stirring constantly.

4 Pack the spinach firmly into 2 ramekins, leave for 1½ minutes, then turn out onto warmed serving plates.

LEMON SOUFFLÉ CUSTARD

2 eggs, separated
grated rind and juice of 1 lemon
125 g (4 oz) caster sugar
15 g (½ oz) butter
25 g (1 oz) plain flour
250 ml (8 fl oz) milk

To Decorate:
icing sugar, for sprinkling
shredded rind of ½ lemon
mint sprig

1 Put the egg yolks, lemon rind and juice, sugar, butter and flour in a bowl and beat well. Add the milk and blend in.

2 Whisk the egg whites until stiff. Stir 15 ml (1 tbsp) into the egg yolk mixture to lighten it, then fold in the remaining egg white.

3 Spoon the mixture into a greased shallow ovenproof dish and place in a bain-marie or roasting pan containing enough hot water to come halfway up the sides of the dish. Cook in a preheated oven at 180°C (350°F) mark 4 for 8-12 minutes, until risen and firm.

4 Sprinkle with icing sugar, and decorate with shredded lemon rind and a sprig of mint to serve.

Contestants
Jessica Davies • Anna Jarman • Nathalie Wild

Panel of Judges
Phil Vickery • Jean Boht • Loyd Grossman

Nathalie Wild's Menu

MAIN COURSE
Fresh Spinach Tagliatelle with Pesto Sauce
Green Salad with Pine Nuts and Pumpkin Seeds
"The spinach tagliatelle was beautifully made" **Loyd**

DESSERT
Chocolate Rum Torte
"It would be hard to get a better chocolate pudding" **Loyd**

Eleven year old Nathalie Wild from Norwich, is a pupil at the Blackdale Middle School. Nathalie's hobbies include playing chess and candle-making. She is also a nature lover at heart, and enjoys a spot of pond-dipping.

SPINACH TAGLIATELLE WITH PESTO SAUCE

15 g (½ oz) spinach
175 g (6 oz) durum wheat or strong plain flour
1 egg, beaten
7 g (¼ tsp) salt
dash of olive oil

Pesto Sauce:
1 clove garlic, crushed
45 ml (3 tbsp) finely chopped basil
30 ml (2 tbsp) chopped parsley
25 g (1 oz) pine nuts
25 g (1 oz) freshly grated Parmesan cheese
75 ml (2½ fl oz) olive oil
freshly ground black pepper

To Garnish:
toasted pine nuts
black olives (optional)

1 Place the spinach in a food processor and work until finely chopped. Add the flour, egg, salt and oil and mix or pulse until a dough is formed. Transfer to a floured surface and knead lightly until smooth. Wrap in cling film and leave to rest for 15-20 minutes.

2 Divide the dough into 3 pieces and flatten each one into a strip, about 5 mm (¼ inch) thick. Fold in half.

3 Feed the dough repeatedly through a pasta machine, gradually narrowing the setting by one notch each time, until the desired thickness is reached. Fit the tagliatelle cutters and pass each piece of dough through. Place the pasta strips on a clean tea-towel and leave to dry for at least 10 minutes.

4 To prepare the pesto sauce, put all of the ingredients in a blender and work until smooth.

5 Cook the pasta in a large pan of lightly salted boiling water for 3-5 minutes or until 'al dente'. Drain thoroughly and turn into a warmed serving dish. Add the pesto sauce and toss before serving, garnished with the toasted pine nuts, and black olives if wished. Serve with a green salad (see page 105).

GREEN SALAD WITH PINE NUTS AND PUMPKIN SEEDS

selection of green salad leaves, eg
   rocket, iceberg, butterhead, endive
¼ cucumber
25 g (1 oz) pine nuts (approximately)
25 g (1 oz) pumpkin seeds
   (approximately), roasted
few black olives (optional)
chopped oregano, to taste

Dressing:
10 ml (2 tsp) wholegrain mustard
2.5 ml (½ tsp) salt
freshly ground black pepper
5 ml (1 tsp) red wine vinegar or cider
   vinegar
22.5 ml (1½ tbsp) extra-virgin olive oil

1 Tear the salad leaves and put into a salad bowl. Groove the cucumber skin, using a canelle knife, then cut into thick slices. Add to the bowl and mix well. Add the pine nuts and pumpkin seeds.

2 To make the dressing, mix the mustard, salt, pepper and vinegar together in a bowl. Gradually whisk in the oil. Pour the dressing over the salad just before serving and toss lightly.

3 Scatter the olives, if using, and oregano over the salad to serve.

CHOCOLATE RUM TORTE

225 g (8 oz) plain chocolate
37.5 ml (2½ tbsp) liquid glucose
37.5 ml (2½ tbsp) rum
300 ml (½ pint) double cream
40 g (1½ oz) amaretti biscuits, crushed

To Serve:
thick pouring cream
cocoa powder, for dusting
few raspberries (optional)

1 Melt the chocolate in a heatproof bowl over a pan of hot water. Stir in the glucose and rum, then leave to cool.

3 Whip the cream until slightly thickened. Fold into the chocolate mixture.

4 Crush the amaretti biscuits between 2 sheets of greaseproof paper, using a rolling pin. Spread over the bases of 2 individual heart-shaped tins. Spoon the chocolate cream on top, tapping the tins to smooth out the mixture. Chill in the refrigerator overnight or in the freezer for about 1 hour.

5 To serve, spread a pool of cream on each of 2 serving plates. Run a palette knife around the edge of each torte and turn out onto the cream. Dust with cocoa powder to serve. Decorate the edge of each plate with a few raspberries if desired.

The First Semi-Final

Contestants

Jenna Tinson • Ben Domb • Jenny Smith

Panel of Judges

Anton Edelmann • Jane Asher • Loyd Grossman

WINNER

Jenna Tinson's Menu

MAIN COURSE

Stuffed Breast of Chicken with Orange and Tarragon Sauce

Glazed Sugar Snap Peas and Green Beans

Jerusalem Artichoke and Potato Rösti

"It was a very balanced meal. I thought the chicken was lovely, and the stuffing with the nuts I found delicious" **Anton Edelmann**

DESSERT

Coconut Cream Custards with a Mango and Malibu Sauce

"The coconut cream was a delight" **Anton Edelmann**

STUFFED BREAST OF CHICKEN WITH ORANGE AND TARRAGON SAUCE

*2 chicken breast fillets, each about
150 g (5 oz)*

Stuffing:
*25 g (1 oz) butter
1 shallot, finely chopped
1 rasher of smoked bacon, derinded
and chopped
40 g (1½ oz) mushrooms, finely
chopped
30 ml (2 tbsp) pine nuts*

Orange and Tarragon Sauce:
*20 g (¾ oz) butter
1 shallot, finely chopped
90 ml (3 fl oz) white wine
60 ml (2 fl oz) double cream
juice of 1 orange
salt and freshly ground black pepper
10-15 ml (2-3 tsp) chopped tarragon,
to taste*

To Garnish:
*½ orange
40 g (1½ oz) caster sugar
squeeze of lemon juice*

1 First, prepare the stuffing. Melt half of the butter in a pan, add the shallot, cover and sweat for 3-4 minutes until softened. Add the bacon and mushrooms and cook for a few minutes until tender. Stir in the pine nuts and sauté briefly.

2 Cut a pocket horizontally through one side of each chicken breast and fill with the prepared stuffing. Melt the remaining butter in a frying pan, add the chicken, skin-side down, and fry gently, until golden. Turn and lightly brown the other side. Transfer to a baking tray and cook in a preheated oven at 200°C (400°F) mark 6 for 15 minutes or until tender.

3 Meanwhile, prepare the garnish. Finely pare the rind from the orange using a zester. Blanch in plenty of boiling water for 10 minutes to remove all the bitterness. Drain and refresh under cold running water, then cut into strips.

4 Dissolve the sugar in 90 ml (3 fl oz) water in a pan, over a low heat, then increase the heat and boil without stirring for 1 minute. Add the orange rind and lemon juice and boil for about 3 minutes. Remove the orange rind with a slotted spoon and leave to cool.

5 To prepare the sauce, melt half of the butter in a pan, add the shallot, cover and sweat for 2 minutes. Add the wine and reduce by half over a moderate heat. Add 30 ml (1 fl oz) water, the cream and orange juice and heat until slightly thickened. Pass through a sieve, then return to the pan and whisk in the remaining butter. Season with salt and pepper and add the tarragon to taste.

6 Place the chicken on warmed serving plates, surround with the sauce and garnish with the orange zest strips.

GLAZED SUGAR SNAP PEAS AND GREEN BEANS

10 sugar snap peas
10 green beans
15 ml (1 tbsp) salt
knob of butter

1 Place the vegetables in a pan, cover with plenty of boiling water, add the salt and boil, uncovered, for 3 minutes. Drain and refresh under cold running water.

2 Place the butter and 60 ml (4 tbsp) water in a pan and bring to the boil. Add the vegetables, cover and cook for 1 minute, then uncover and cook for a further 1 minute until glazed.

JERUSALEM ARTICHOKE AND POTATO RÖSTI

2 Jerusalem artichokes, peeled
3 small King Edward potatoes, peeled
salt and freshly ground black pepper
75 g (3 oz) clarified butter (see below)

CLARIFIED BUTTER

To prepare the clarified butter, melt the butter in a pan, then skim the scum off the surface. Leave to cool and allow the sediment to settle. Carefully pour off the clarified butter, leaving the sediment behind.

1 Place the vegetables in a pan, cover with boiling water, then simmer for 8 minutes. Drain and leave to cool completely.

2 Grate the vegetables onto a board and season with salt and pepper to taste. Using your fingers, mould the mixture into 4 metal rings, about 7.5 cm (3 inches) in diameter.

3 Heat the clarified butter in a frying pan, carefully position the vegetable rösti (in the rings) in the pan and fry until the underside is golden. Remove the metal rings, turn the rösti and continue to fry until cooked through and golden brown.

COCONUT CREAM CUSTARDS WITH A MANGO AND MALIBU SAUCE

125 ml (4 fl oz) milk
45 ml (3 tbsp) coconut powder
90 ml (3 fl oz) double cream
pinch of salt
3 egg yolks
30 ml (2 tbsp) caster sugar

Mango Sauce:
1 ripe mango
1 nectarine
3 apricots
juice of ½ lemon
30 ml (2 tbsp) icing sugar
15 ml (1 tbsp) Malibu

1 Put a roasting tin containing 2.5 cm (1 inch) of water into the oven. Heat the oven to 160°C (325°F) mark 3.

2 Warm the milk in a pan, add the coconut powder and stir until dissolved. Add the cream and heat slowly. Add the salt and remove from the heat.

3 Whisk the egg yolks and sugar together thoroughly, then whisk into the coconut mixture a little at a time.

4 Divide the mixture between 2 well greased ramekins. Stand them in the roasting tin and cook for 40 minutes.

5 Meanwhile, prepare the sauce. Peel and slice the mango, nectarine and apricots, discarding the stones. Put into a blender or food processor with the lemon juice, icing sugar and Malibu. Work until smooth, then pass through a nylon sieve.

6 Carefully remove the roasting tin from the oven. Allow to cool slightly before taking out the ramekins.

7 To serve, turn the custards out onto individual serving plates and accompany with the sauce.

The First Semi-Final

Contestants
Jenna Tinson • Ben Domb • Jenny Smith

Panel of Judges
Anton Edelmann • Jane Asher • Loyd Grossman

Ben Domb's Menu

MAIN COURSE

Poussin in a Cheesy Cream and Green Peppercorn Sauce

Potatoes with Fresh Herbs

Glazed Shallots

Asparagus

"I think the sauce was very nice. He cooked it awfully nicely, his asparagus was lovely" **Anton Edelmann**

DESSERT

Morello Cherry and Nut Parcels

"Very tasty" **Jane Asher**

POUSSIN IN A CHEESY CREAM AND GREEN PEPPERCORN SAUCE

15 ml (1 tbsp) olive oil
1 poussin, cut into 4 pieces
2.5 ml (½ tsp) salt
2.5 ml (½ tsp) freshly grated nutmeg
30 ml (2 tbsp) green peppercorns
rosemary sprig
300 ml (½ pint) double cream
2.5 ml (½ tsp) brandy
black olives, to garnish

1 Heat the olive oil in a pan, add the poussin pieces and cook until browned. Add the salt, nutmeg, 15 ml (1 tbsp) peppercorns and rosemary. Add water to a depth of 2.5 cm (1 inch) and simmer for 50 minutes.

2 Remove the poussin pieces and set aside. Add the remaining peppercorns and the cream to the pan and heat, without boiling, until reduced slightly.

3 Return the poussin pieces to the pan and turn to coat with the sauce. Add the brandy and simmer for 5 minutes.

4 Serve garnished with olives and accompanied by the vegetables (see pages 114-5).

GLAZED SHALLOTS

6 shallots, peeled
45 ml (3 tbsp) wine vinegar
7.5 ml (1½ tsp) sugar
45 ml (3 tbsp) oil
6 cloves
2 bay leaves
2.5 ml (½ tsp) salt

1 Place all the ingredients in a small pan, bring to the boil and simmer, stirring occasionally, for about 20 minutes, until the onions soften.

2 Discard the cloves and bay leaves before serving.

COOK'S NOTE

Diced carrots, red peppers, celery and mushrooms can be cooked with the shallots for a vegetable medley.

POTATOES WITH FRESH HERBS

2 large potatoes, unpeeled
45 ml (3 tbsp) olive oil
3 cloves garlic, crushed
few conserved red peppers (optional)
4 basil leaves, chopped
2 sage leaves, chopped
salt and freshly ground black pepper
a little single cream

1 Microwave the potatoes on high for 15 minutes, until soft. Leave to cool, then cut in half and scoop out the flesh into a bowl; set the skins aside, if required.

2 Heat the oil in a pan, add the garlic, red peppers (if using) and half of the herbs and fry gently for a few seconds. Mix in to the potato, then press through a sieve. Add the cream, salt and pepper to taste and the rest of the herbs and stir well until smooth. Spoon back into the skins (if using) to serve.

ASPARAGUS

16 asparagus spears
½ lemon
pinch of salt

1 Trim the asparagus stalks, then add to a pan of boiling water with the lemon and salt. Cook for 8 minutes, until tender but still firm and crisp.

2 Drain the asparagus and refresh for 1 second under cold running water. Heat through briefly if necessary to serve.

MORELLO CHERRY AND NUT PARCELS

175 g (6 oz) butter
225 g (8 oz) filo pastry (approximately 12 sheets)
125 g (4 oz) breadcrumbs
125 g (4 oz) caster sugar
5 ml (1 tsp) freshly grated nutmeg
ground cinnamon, to taste
125 g (4 oz) shelled walnuts, roughly chopped
½-⅔ x 680 g (1½ lb) jar of pitted morello cherries, drained
1 egg, beaten

To Serve:
icing sugar, for dusting
125 g (4 oz) Greek-style yogurt

1 Melt 50 g (2 oz) of the butter. Lay one sheet of filo pastry on a large square of foil. Brush with melted butter. Lay 5 more sheets on top, brushing each with melted butter, building up a square. Repeat with the remaining filo sheets to make another square.

2 Melt the remaining butter in a large pan. Add the breadcrumbs, sugar, nutmeg, cinnamon, walnuts and half of the cherries; mix well. Put 2 large spoonfuls of mixture on each filo square.

3 Fold over the top right and bottom left hand corners, from about halfway along the sides, in towards the centre. Fold the triangular pieces of pastry in half again by folding the point back. Fold the remaining corners in to the centre, then back in the same way to enclose the filling and form a parcel.

4 Brush very gently with beaten egg and bake in a preheated oven at 190°C (375°F) mark 5 for 15-20 minutes, until puffy and golden.

5 Meanwhile make the cherry coulis. Purée the remaining cherries in a blender or food processor, then pass through a nylon sieve.

6 Remove the filo parcels from the oven and sprinkle generously with icing sugar. Place on individual serving plates and surround with the cherry coulis and yogurt. Serve at once.

The First Semi-Final

Contestants

Jenna Tinson • Ben Domb • Jenny Smith

Panel of Judges

Anton Edelmann • Jane Asher • Loyd Grossman

Jenny Smith's Menu

MAIN COURSE

Chicken with a Prune and Walnut Stuffing

Basmati Rice

Broccoli

"I loved the whole combination of the dish" **Anton Edelmann**

DESSERT

Rich Lemon and Lime Ice Cream in a Brandy Snap Basket

"The ice cream was a triumph. I thought it was wonderful" **Jane Asher**

CHICKEN WITH A PRUNE AND WALNUT STUFFING

15 ml (1 tbsp) sunflower oil
½ onion, chopped
50 g (2 oz) 'no-need-to-soak' prunes
25 g (1 oz) chopped walnuts
1 clove garlic, crushed
7.5 ml (1½ tsp) lemon juice
2 large chicken thighs, skinned and boned
4 rashers of streaky bacon, derinded
120 ml (4 fl oz) chicken stock (approximately)

1 Heat the oil in a pan, add the onion and fry until brown. Snip the prunes into small pieces with scissors. Remove the pan from the heat, add the walnuts, prunes, garlic and lemon juice and stir well.

2 Place each piece of chicken on top of 2 rashers of bacon. Fill the bone cavity with the prune mixture. Wrap the bacon tightly around the thighs to enclose the stuffing and secure with a wooden cocktail stick. Place in a small casserole dish and pour in enough chicken stock to cover the base and moisten the chicken.

3 Cook in a preheated oven at 190°C (375°F) mark 5 for about 45 minutes, until the bacon is brown and the chicken is cooked through. Check from time to time that the liquid hasn't totally evaporated, adding a little extra stock if necessary.

4 Cut the stuffed chicken thighs into thick slices to serve. Accompany with Basmati rice and broccoli.

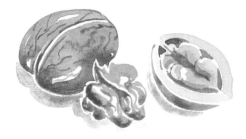

RICH LEMON AND LIME ICE CREAM IN BRANDY SNAP BASKETS

2 egg yolks
50 g (2 oz) caster sugar, plus 15 ml
  (1 tbsp)
1 lemon
75 ml (5 tbsp) double cream
juice of 1 lime

Brandy Snap Baskets:
25 g (1 oz) butter, softened
25 g (1 oz) granulated sugar
25 g (1 oz) plain flour
5 ml (1 tsp) ground ginger
15 ml (1 tbsp) golden syrup

To Decorate (optional):
frosted fruit and flowers (see below)

COOK'S TIP

To prepare the frosted fruit and flowers, brush lightly with egg white, then sprinkle with caster sugar and leave to dry.

1 Place the egg yolks and 50 g (2 oz) sugar in a bowl and beat with an electric whisk until thick and creamy-white in colour.

2 Remove strips of rind from the lemon, using a zester, then squeeze the juice. Set aside the rind.

3 Place the cream in a bowl and add 15 ml (1 tbsp) each lemon and lime juice. Beat until thick, but take care not to over-beat or the mixture may curdle. Fold into the egg and sugar mixture.

4 Transfer to a freezerproof container and freeze until firm, whisking 2 or 3 times during freezing to break down the ice crystals and ensure an even-textured result.

5 Meanwhile, make the brandy snap baskets. Cream the butter and sugar together in a bowl. Sift in the flour and ginger, then add the syrup. Mix until well blended.

6 Place 2 marble size 'blobs' well apart on a non-stick baking sheet and bake in a preheated oven at 190°C (375°F) mark 5 for 7-8 minutes, until golden brown and lacy. Leave for a few seconds, then carefully remove from the baking sheet with a fish slice and mould each one over the base of an uptuned jam jar to form a basket shape. Leave to cool and set.

7 Meanwhile, place the remaining 15 ml (1 tbsp) sugar in a pan with 15 ml (1 tbsp) each lemon and lime juice. Heat gently until the sugar has dissolved, then add the reserved lemon rind and poach gently for about 5 minutes, until softened.

8 To serve, scoop the ice cream into the brandy baskets and decorate with the lemon rind and frosted flowers and leaves, if wished.

── The Second Semi-Final ──

Contestants
Ross Spence • Robyn Hardy • Cathy Merrick

Panel of Judges
Josceline Dimbleby • Paul Nicholas • Loyd Grossman

WINNER

Ross Spence's Menu

MAIN COURSE

Roasted Loin of Lamb in a Herb Crust on a Parsnip Galette, served with a light Madeira Sauce

Glazed Carrots and Shallots

"I've hardly ever tasted such tender lamb – it was absolutely wonderful" **Josceline Dimbleby**

DESSERT

Apple Charlotte, with a Mascarpone and Nutmeg Ice Cream and Calvados Sauce

"That nutmeg ice cream was wonderful" **Loyd**

ROASTED LOIN OF LAMB IN A HERB CRUST ON A PARSNIP GALETTE

4 slices of bread, crusts removed
2 parsley sprigs
2 rosemary sprigs
salt and freshly ground black pepper
25 g (1 oz) clarified butter (see
    page 10)
2 lamb fillets (loin), each about 175 g
    (6 oz)
wholegrain mustard, to taste

Parsnip Galette:
50 g (2 oz) clarified butter (see
    page 110)
1 parsnip
1 potato

Madeira Sauce:
5 ml (1 tsp) butter
2 shallots, chopped
5 ml (1 tsp) brown sugar
parsnip and potato trimmings (from
    galette)
rosemary stalks (from sprigs)
50 ml (2 fl oz) Madeira
300 ml (½ pint) lamb stock

To Garnish:
rosemary sprigs

1 Put the bread, herbs and salt and pepper in a food processor and work until fine crumbs are formed.

2 Melt half of the butter in a heavy-based non-stick frying pan. Season the lamb with salt and pepper, add to the pan and brown quickly on both sides and ends to seal. Remove from the pan and dry on kitchen paper. Spread one side of each fillet with mustard, then cover with the breadcrumbs. Melt the remaining butter in the non-stick pan until very hot, then add the lamb, crumbed-side down, and fry quickly until golden. Transfer to a baking tray, crumbed-side up, and set aside.

3 To make the galette, peel and grate the parsnip and potato. Mix together and season with salt and pepper. Heat the clarified butter in the non-stick pan and add the parsnip and potato, flattening the mixture into a cake but without squeezing out the vegetable juices. Cook quickly, turning once, until browned on both sides.

4 Place the galette on the baking tray with the lamb and cook in a preheated oven at 150°C (300°F) mark 2 for 8 minutes; the lamb should still be pink.

5 Meanwhile, prepare the sauce. Melt the butter in a pan, add the shallots, sugar, vegetable trimmings and rosemary stalks; cover and sweat for about 2 minutes. Add the Madeira and cook, uncovered, until reduced by half. Add the lamb stock and reduce again by half. Season with salt and pepper to taste. Strain and keep warm.

6 To serve, place the galette on a warmed serving plate. Slice the lamb, arrange on top and garnish with rosemary. Pour the sauce around the galette and serve with glazed shallots and carrots, sprinkled with parsley.

APPLE CHARLOTTE WITH A MASCARPONE AND NUTMEG ICE CREAM AND CALVADOS SAUCE

Ice Cream:
2 egg yolks
50 g (2 oz) icing sugar, sifted
250 g (9 oz) mascarpone cheese
5 ml (1 tsp) vanilla essence
freshly grated nutmeg, to taste

Charlotte:
6 slices of bread, crusts removed
50 g (2 oz) butter, melted
25 g (1 oz) sultanas
2 cooking apples, peeled, cored and
   sliced
ground cinnamon, to taste
40 g (1½ oz) brown sugar
   (approximately)

Sauce:
150 ml (¼ pint) milk
150 ml (¼ pint) double cream
1 vanilla pod
3 egg yolks
75 g (3 oz) caster sugar
dash of Calvados

To Decorate:
4 black grapes, sliced
2 large strawberries, sliced

1 First make the ice cream. Whisk together the egg yolks and icing sugar. Add the mascarpone and beat well. Add the vanilla essence and grated nutmeg to taste. Turn into a freezerproof container and freeze until firm, beating 2 or 3 times during freezing to break down the ice crystals and ensure an even-textured result.

2 To prepare the charlotte, roll the slices of bread thinly, cut into fingers and use to line 2 ramekin dishes, making sure there are no spaces between the bread fingers and leaving the ends overhanging. Brush liberally with melted butter.

3 Heat a little of the butter in a pan, add the sultanas and cook gently until 'plump'. Add the apples, cinnamon and sugar to taste; stir to coat well. Transfer to the ramekins. Brush the overhanging bread with butter and fold over the apple to enclose completely. Cook in a preheated oven at 180°C (350°F) mark 4 for about 20 minutes.

4 To make the sauce, put the milk, cream and vanilla pod in a pan and bring slowly to the boil, to infuse. Whisk the egg yolks and sugar together in a bowl, then pour on the hot milk and cream, whisking constantly. Pour back into the pan and cook, stirring, until thick enough to coat the back of a wooden spoon; do not allow to boil. Pass through a fine sieve. Stir in the Calvados to taste.

5 To serve, turn out the charlottes onto individual serving plates and surround with the sauce. Decorate with the grapes and strawberries. Serve with the ice cream.

The Second Semi-Final

Contestants

Ross Spence • Robyn Hardy • Cathy Merrick

Panel of Judges

Josceline Dimbleby • Paul Nicholas • Loyd Grossman

Robyn Hardy's Menu

MAIN COURSE

Weeping Lamb with Potato and Onion

Mixed Green Salad

"The lamb was good and I thought the potatoes were terribly good"
Josceline Dimbleby

DESSERT

Apple Tart, served with Brandy Cream

"The pastry was a triumph" **Josceline Dimbleby**

WEEPING LAMB WITH POTATO AND ONION

1 kg (2 lb) knuckle end leg of lamb
1 clove garlic, cut into slivers
few rosemary sprigs
15 g (½ oz) butter
15 ml (1 tbsp) olive oil
2 potatoes, sliced
1 onion, sliced
salt and freshly ground black pepper
150-300 ml (¼-½ pint) vegetable stock

1 Slash the lamb in several places with a sharp knife and insert the garlic and rosemary. Rub all over with the butter. Place in a roasting dish and pour over the olive oil. Cook in a preheated oven at 220°C (425°F) mark 7 for 15 minutes.

2 Remove the meat from the dish. Arrange the potatoes and onion in the dish, season well and make sure they are thoroughly coated in oil. Pour over the stock.

3 Stand a roasting rack in the dish over the vegetables and place the meat on it, so that the fat will drip onto them. Return to the oven and cook for 30 minutes. Remove the lamb, cover and leave to rest in a warm place. Return the vegetables to the oven for a further 10 minutes.

4 Carve the meat into slices and serve with the vegetables and juices, accompanied by a green salad.

APPLE TART

Pastry:
75 g (3 oz) self-raising flour, sifted
5 ml (1 tsp) icing sugar
pinch of salt
50 g (2 oz) unsalted butter
1 egg, beaten with 15 ml (1 tbsp) water

Filling:
225 g (8 oz) cooking apples
40 g (1½ oz) caster sugar
60 ml (2 fl oz) single cream
7.5 ml (½ tsp) plain flour
2.5 ml (½ tsp) vanilla essence

To Serve:
whipped cream, flavoured with a little
    brandy

1 First make the pastry. Place the flour, icing sugar and salt in a bowl and stir to mix. Rub in the butter until the mixture resembles breadcrumbs. Add the beaten egg, a tablespoon at a time, to bind the dough until it forms a ball; you should only need to use half of the egg. Wrap in cling film and chill in the refrigerator for 15 minutes.

2 Roll out the pastry on a floured surface and use to line a 15 cm (6 inch) flan dish. Line with foil and baking beans and bake blind in a preheated oven at 220°C (425°F) mark 7 for 10 minutes. Leave to cool slightly, then remove the foil and beans.

3 Peel the apples, cut into quarters and remove the cores. Cut each quarter into 3 slices and arrange in the pastry case. Lower the oven temperature to 200°C (400°F) mark 6 and bake the flan for 10 minutes.

4 Mix the sugar, cream, flour and vanilla essence together in a bowl. Pour over the apples and return to the oven at 180°C (350°F) mark 4 for 20 minutes or until the cream is set.

5 Serve hot or cold, with whipped cream flavoured with a little brandy.

The Second Semi-Final

Contestants
Ross Spence • Robyn Hardy • Cathy Merrick

Panel of Judges
Josceline Dimbleby • Paul Nicholas • Loyd Grossman

Cathy Merrick's Menu

MAIN COURSE

Squid Ink Fettucine, with Mediterranean Seafood Sauce and Lime
Fennel Salad with Ciabatta Croûtons

*"It was a lovely delicate meal. I thought her pasta was brilliant...
nobody could have made nicer pasta"* **Josceline Dimbleby**

DESSERT

Mascarpone and Amaretto Dessert with Apricot Sauce

"Really delicious" **Josceline Dimbleby**

SQUID INK FETTUCINE WITH MEDITERRANEAN SEAFOOD SAUCE AND LIME

Pasta:
100 g (3½ oz) plain flour
pinch of salt
1 egg (size 3)
1 sachet squid ink

Seafood Sauce:
450 ml (¾ pint) fish stock
50 g (2 oz) cleaned squid, sliced
175 g (6 oz) monkfish, cubed
50 g (2 oz) cleaned scallops
25 ml (1 fl oz) Soave or other white
* wine*
15 ml (1 tbsp) lime juice
125 ml (4 fl oz) crème fraîche

To Garnish:
2 limes
few fennel fronds

1 First make the pasta. Sift the flour and salt into a bowl and make a well in the centre. Add the egg and squid ink. Using a fork, gently beat the egg and squid ink together in the well, then gradually draw in the flour and mix to a rough dough. Use your hands to bring the dough together. Knead on a floured board for 5 minutes until smooth, then wrap in cling film and leave to rest for 30 minutes.

2 Meanwhile, prepare the sauce. Place the fish stock and squid in a pan, bring to simmering point and poach gently for 20-30 minutes, adding the monkfish and scallops for the last 5 minutes. Drain and set aside.

3 Pass the pasta repeatedly through a pasta machine to roll out, narrowing the setting by one notch each time until the required thickness is reached. Fit the fettucine cutters and pass the pasta through to cut into noodles. Leave to dry on a clean tea-towel for 30 minutes.

4 To finish the sauce, place the wine and lime juice in a pan and bring to the boil. Add the crème fraîche and boil until reduced by half. Add the fish and keep warm.

5 Cook the pasta in a large pan of boiling salted water for 3-5 minutes, until *'al dente'*. Drain well and arrange on 2 warmed serving plates. Spoon the seafood sauce into a 'nest' in the centre. Garnish with lime slices, strips of lime rind and fennel fronds. Serve with the fennel salad (see page 128).

FENNEL SALAD WITH CIABATTA CROÛTONS

1 fennel bulb
15 ml (1 tbsp) olive oil
2 slices of ciabatta, cubed
assorted salad leaves, eg frisée, lollo
*   biando, rocket*

Dressing:
2.5 ml (½ tsp) fennel seeds
5 ml (1 tsp) lime juice
5 ml (1 tsp) fennel vinegar
30 ml (2 tbsp) olive oil
salt and freshly ground black pepper

To Garnish:
fennel sprigs

1 Thinly slice the fennel vertically, discarding the core, then separate the slices into moon-shaped pieces. Immerse in a bowl of cold water and leave to soak while preparing the croûtons and dressing.

2 Heat the oil in a pan, add the bread cubes and fry until golden. Drain on kitchen paper.

3 To make the dressing, crush the fennel seeds using a pestle and mortar. Add the lime juice and vinegar, then whisk in the oil. Season with salt and pepper to taste.

4 Drain the fennel slices and place in a bowl with the prepared salad leaves. Pour over the dressing just before serving and toss to mix.

5 Arrange the salad on 2 small plates and top with the croûtons. Garnish with fennel sprigs.

MASCARPONE AND AMARETTO DESSERT WITH APRICOT SAUCE

25 g (1 oz) amaretti biscuits
15 g (1/2 oz) butter, melted
40 g (1 1/2 oz) caster sugar
25 g (1 oz) almonds, toasted
75 g (3 oz) mascarpone cheese
15 ml (1 tbsp) amaretto di Saronno
   liqueur
1 egg white

Apricot Sauce:

125 g (4 oz) ready-to-eat dried apricots
15 g (1/2 oz) caster sugar
30 ml (2 tbsp) apricot brandy

To Decorate:

apricot slices
mint sprigs
15 ml (1 tbsp) double cream

1 Crush the amaretti biscuits between 2 sheets of greaseproof paper, using a rolling pin. Mix the amaretti crumbs with the melted butter and press into two 7.5 cm (3 inch) ring moulds, placed on a serving plate. Chill until required.

2 Place 25 g (1 oz) sugar in a pan; add 10 ml (2 tsp) water and heat gently until dissolved, then bring to the boil and cook to a golden brown caramel. Carefully stir in the almonds, then pour onto a greased baking sheet and leave to cool and harden.

3 Whisk the mascarpone and liqueur together in one bowl. Whisk the egg white in another bowl until soft peaks form, then whisk in the remaining sugar. Fold the two mixtures together.

4 Crush the praline between 2 sheets of greaseproof paper, using a rolling pin. Add half to the mascarpone mixture, then spoon over the biscuit bases and spread evenly. Chill while making the sauce.

5 Simmer the apricots in water to cover for 20 minutes. Place in a food processor and work until smooth, then rub through a fine sieve.

6 Place the sugar in a pan, add 60 ml (2 fl oz) water, bring to the boil and boil for 1 minute.

7 Add the brandy to the apricot purée, then stir in the sugar syrup to thin the sauce. Chill until required.

8 To serve, carefully remove the rings from the desserts and surround with the apricot sauce. Dot the sauce with cream and feather it out with a cocktail stick. Decorate with apricot slices and mint sprigs. Serve at once.

The Third Semi-Final

Contestants

Jessica Davies • Ashley Temple • Kate Watkins

Panel of Judges

Paul Heathcote • Emma Forbes • Loyd Grossman

WINNER

Jessica Davies' Menu

MAIN COURSE

Gingered Chicken with an Orange Sauce

Wild Rice

Broccoli with Almonds

"I loved the chicken, the flavours were fantastic" **Emma Forbes**

DESSERT

Minted Strawberries in Rosé Syrup

"The dessert was supreme... it was a good marriage" **Paul Heathcote**

GINGERED CHICKEN WITH AN ORANGE SAUCE

2 chicken breasts, each about 150 g
* (5 oz)*
15 ml (1 tbsp) oil
1 clove garlic, crushed
25 g (1 oz) fresh root ginger, grated
6-8 spring onions, trimmed and cut into
* 2.5 cm (1 inch) pieces*
juice of 2 oranges
300 ml (½ pint) chicken stock
15 g (½ oz) cornflour (optional)

To Garnish:
spring onion curls (see below)
orange slices

1 Slice the chicken breasts into slivers.

2 Heat the oil in a frying pan, add the garlic and ginger and fry gently for about 1 minute.

3 Add the chicken and cook for 3-4 minutes, then add the spring onions and cook for a further 2 minutes. Add the orange juice and stock and simmer gently for about 2 minutes. Transfer the chicken to a warmed serving dish.

4 If necessary, thicken the sauce with blended cornflour: blend to a paste with a little water, add to the sauce and cook, stirring, until thickened.

5 Pour the sauce over the chicken and garnish with spring onion curls and orange slices. Serve with wild rice and broccoli.

COOK'S TIP

To make spring onion curls, trim the onions, then shred the green end with a sharp knife, leaving 2.5 cm (1 inch) attached at the base. Immerse in a bowl of iced water until they curl, then drain.

MINTED STRAWBERRIES IN ROSÉ SYRUP

125 ml (4 fl oz) sweet rosé wine
125 g (4 oz) caster sugar
few mint leaves
175 g (6 oz) large ripe strawberries, halved
finely shredded strips of lemon rind, blanched
a little sugar, for coating

1 Place the wine and sugar in a pan, with the mint leaves. Stir over a low heat until the sugar has dissolved, then increase the heat and boil, without stirring, for 1 minute. Strain the syrup, discarding the mint.

2 Pour the syrup onto 2 serving plates, to form a pool. Arrange the strawberries in the syrup.

3 Toss the lemon rind in sugar to coat and sprinkle over the strawberries. Serve with whipped cream.

The Third Semi-Final

Contestants
Jessica Davies • Ashley Temple • Kate Watkins

Panel of Judges
Paul Heathcote • Emma Forbes • Loyd Grossman

Ashley Temple's Menu

MAIN COURSE
Fillets of Plaice with a Piquant Tartare Sauce
Gâteau d'Aubergine with a Fresh Tomato Sauce
Jersey Royal New Potatoes tossed in Butter
"I loved the gâteau of aubergine" **Emma Forbes**

DESSERT
Chocolate Purgatory Pudding, served with a Vanilla Sauce
"The sauces were delicious" **Emma Forbes**

FILLETS OF PLAICE WITH A PIQUANT TARTARE SAUCE

2 fillets of plaice, skinned
25 g (1 oz) Cheddar cheese, grated
50 g (2 oz) breadcrumbs
pinch of cayenne pepper

Tartare Sauce:
1 egg, plus 1 egg yolk
2.5 ml (½ tsp) Dijon mustard
300 ml (½ pint) groundnut oil
30 ml (2 tbsp) lemon juice
15 ml (1 tbsp) capers, chopped
3 small gherkins, chopped
salt and freshly ground black pepper

1 First make the tartare sauce. Beat the egg, egg yolk and mustard together in a bowl. Add the oil very very slowly – a drop at a time – whisking thoroughly between each addition, to make a mayonnaise. As it thickens, add the oil in a slow steady stream, whisking constantly. Beat in the lemon juice, then stir in the capers and gherkins, and season to taste with salt and pepper.

2 Cook the fish under a preheated medium grill for about 3 minutes, turning once.

3 Meanwhile, mix together the cheese, breadcrumbs and cayenne.

4 Spread the tartare sauce over the fish, then dip in the breadcrumb mixture to coat. Return to the grill for 3-5 minutes until golden brown and bubbling. Serve with Gâteau d'Aubergine (see page 135) and new potatoes.

GÂTEAU D'AUBERGINE

½ aubergine, thickly sliced
olive oil, for cooking
3 ripe plum tomatoes
a little chopped thyme
salt
200 g (7 oz) young spinach leaves
1 garlic clove, halved
a knob of butter
1 courgette, thinly sliced
few basil leaves, chopped

Tomato Sauce:
6 tomatoes
few basil leaves
a little olive oil
salt and freshly ground black pepper

COOK'S TIP

For these vegetable gâteaux, you will need two 6.5 cm (2½ inch) lengths of plastic drainpipe, each about 7 cm (2¾ inch) in diameter. Your local plumber or builder's merchant should be able to supply these. Make sure the cling film is suitable for use in the microwave.

---

1 Score the aubergine skin with a sharp knife. Heat a little olive oil in a heavy-based frying pan and fry the aubergine slices for 2 minutes on each side. Transfer to a baking tin and place in a preheated oven at 190°C (375°F) mark 5.

2 Peel, quarter and deseed the tomatoes, then add to the baking tin and sprinkle with thyme, salt and a little olive oil.

3 Place the spinach in a pan with just the water clinging to the leaves after washing, the garlic and a knob of butter. Cook until just wilted. Discard the garlic.

4 Meanwhile, sauté the courgettes in a little olive oil for 2-3 minutes. Drain on kitchen paper.

5 Line two pieces of drainpipe (see left) with cling film and pierce 5 holes in the cling film. Layer the spinach in the base of the rings, then line the sides with the courgette slices. Fill with the tomatoes, adding the chopped basil leaves. Cover with the aubergine slices.

6 Cover the tops with kitchen paper and weight down. Leave to drain for 20-30 minutes.

7 Meanwhile, make the tomato sauce. Purée the tomatoes and basil leaves in a blender or food processor. Pass through a sieve into a pan and heat through gently. Whisk in the olive oil and season with salt and pepper to taste.

8 Microwave the gâteaux on high for 2 minutes, then turn out onto warmed serving plates and surround with the tomato sauce.

CHOCOLATE PURGATORY PUDDING WITH VANILLA SAUCE

50 g (2 oz) caster sugar
pinch of ground cinnamon
50 g (2 oz) fine semolina
5 ml (1 tsp) baking powder
70 g (2 3/4 oz) cocoa powder
25 g (1 oz) butter, melted
2 eggs, beaten
50 g (2 oz) mixed Brazils, pistachios,
    walnuts and hazelnuts, roasted and
    roughly chopped
75 g (3 oz) soft dark brown sugar

Vanilla Sauce:
250 ml (8 fl oz) milk
60 ml (2 fl oz) single cream
1/2 vanilla pod
4 egg yolks
50 g (2 oz) sugar

1 Put the caster sugar, cinnamon, semolina, baking powder and 25 g (1 oz) of the cocoa in a bowl and stir together. Make a well in the centre.

2 Add the melted butter to the eggs and beat well, then add to the dry ingredients with the nuts and mix thoroughly.

3 In a separate bowl, blend the remaining cocoa powder and brown sugar with 300 ml (1/2 pint) hot water until smooth.

4 Half-fill well greased individual soufflé dishes with the nut mixture, then top with the cocoa mixture. Bake in a preheated oven at 190°C (375°F) mark 5 for 35 minutes.

5 To make the vanilla sauce, put the milk, cream and vanilla pod in a pan and heat gently to just below boiling point. Remove from the heat and leave to infuse for 10 minutes. Discard the vanilla pod.

6 Whisk the egg yolks and sugar together in a bowl until pale and fluffy. Gradually stir in the warmed milk. Strain back into the pan and heat very gently, stirring constantly, until the sauce thickens.

7 To serve, pool the vanilla sauce on 2 warmed serving plates. Turn out the chocolate puddings onto the sauce and serve at once.

The Third Semi-Final

Contestants
Jessica Davies • Ashley Temple • Kate Watkins

Panel of Judges
Paul Heathcote • Emma Forbes • Loyd Grossman

Kate Watkins' Menu

MAIN COURSE
Chicken Marsala with Apricots

Duchesse Potatoes

Stir-fried Vegetables

"The chicken marsala was nice, and it was seasoned to perfection"
Paul Heathcote

DESSERT
Vanilla Cream Cheese Hearts, with a Raspberry Coulis

"The pudding was just out of this world" **Emma Forbes**

CHICKEN MARSALA WITH APRICOTS

a little oil or unsalted butter, for frying
2 chicken breasts, each about 225 g
  (8 oz)
1 small onion, chopped
125 ml (4 fl oz) Marsala
300 ml (½ pint) double cream
salt and freshly ground black pepper
50 g (2 oz) apricots, stoned

To Garnish:
chopped chives

1 Heat a little oil or butter in a frying pan, add the chicken breasts and fry for 8 minutes on each side, until golden brown. Transfer to a warmed dish, cover and keep warm.

2 Add the onion to the pan and fry until golden brown. Add the Marsala, cream and salt and pepper to taste. Bring to the boil, then lower the heat and simmer until reduced and thickened. Stir in the apricots.

3 Garnish the chicken with chopped chives and serve with the sauce. Accompany with duchesse potatoes and stir-fried vegetables.

VANILLA CREAM CHEESE HEARTS WITH A RASPBERRY COULIS

10 ml (2 tsp) powdered gelatine
200 g (7 oz) Philadelphia cream cheese
200 g (7 oz) fromage frais
10 ml (2 tsp) vanilla essence
30 ml (2 tbsp) icing sugar
150 ml (¼ pint) double cream

Raspberry Coulis:
450 g (1 lb) raspberries
30 ml (2 tbsp) caster sugar

To Decorate:
15 ml (1 tbsp) double cream
4 raspberries

1 Pour 60 ml (2 fl oz) hot water into a small jug, sprinkle on the gelatine and allow to dissolve.

2 Put the cream cheese, fromage frais, vanilla essence and icing sugar in a bowl and whisk until blended. Fold in the cream, then stir in the dissolved gelatine.

3 Divide the mixture between 2 individual lightly oiled heart-shaped moulds and transfer to a freezer for 1 hour, until set.

4 Meanwhile, rub the raspberries through a sieve to make a purée. Stir in the sugar.

5 To serve, turn out the cream cheese hearts onto individual serving plates and surround with the coulis. Dot the raspberry coulis with cream and feather with a cocktail stick. Decorate with the raspberries.

THE FINAL

Junior

● **19** **95** ●

MASTERCHEF

The Final

Contestants

Jenna Tinson • Jessica Davies • Ross Spence

Panel of Judges

Michel Roux Jnr • Terence Conran • Loyd Grossman

WINNER

Jenna Tinson's Menu

MAIN COURSE

Salmon Fillets with Herb Sauce and a Tomato Butter Sauce

Rice Parcels

Asparagus

"The tomato sauce was really excellent with the salmon" **Terence Conran**

DESSERT

Passion Fruit and Citrus Puddings, with a Cointreau Sauce

"That was really good" **Loyd**

SALMON FILLETS WITH HERB SAUCE AND TOMATO BUTTER SAUCE

30 ml (2 tbsp) olive oil
2 salmon fillets, each 150 g (5 oz)
salt and freshly ground black pepper

Herb Sauce:
50 g (2 oz) butter
1 shallot, chopped
60 ml (2 fl oz) white wine
60 ml (2 fl oz) fish stock
90 ml (3 fl oz) double cream
squeeze of lemon juice
2 fennel sprigs

Fresh Tomato Butter Sauce:
300 g (10 oz) tomatoes, roughly
  chopped
2 drops of Worcestershire sauce
2.5 ml ($\frac{1}{2}$ tsp) caster sugar
30 g (1$\frac{1}{4}$ oz) butter

COOK'S TIP
For extra flavour use olive oil flavoured with sun-dried tomatoes to cook the salmon. Toss any leftover spinach (from the rice parcels) in the pan in which the salmon was cooked and serve as an accompaniment.

---

1 First make the herb sauce. Melt 20 g ($\frac{3}{4}$ oz) butter in a pan, add the shallot, cover and sweat gently until softened. Add the wine and cook until reduced by about half. Add the stock and reduce again by about half. Add the cream and reduce a little more. Add salt and pepper to taste, a squeeze of lemon juice, and the fennel. Remove from the heat and leave to stand for about 10 minutes to allow the flavours to develop. Strain through a sieve, reheat gently and whisk in the remaining butter before serving.

2 To make the tomato butter sauce, put the tomatoes, Worcestershire sauce, sugar, salt and pepper in a food processor or blender and work for 20 seconds. Transfer to a bowl and set aside to allow the flavours to combine. Turn into a pan, heat gently, then whisk in the butter just before serving.

3 To cook the salmon, heat the oil in a pan, add the salmon fillets and fry for 1 minute on each side. Transfer to an ovenproof dish and cook in a preheated oven at 180°C (350°F) mark 4 for 3 minutes. (Set aside the pan and dish for cooking the spinach and asparagus accompaniments.)

4 To serve, pour the herb sauce onto 2 warmed serving plates. Arrange the rice parcels (see page 142) in the centre and top with the salmon. Pour over the tomato butter sauce. Serve with asparagus and spinach.

RICE PARCELS

450 ml (¾ pint) mixed fish stock and
  water
50 g (2 oz) mixed long grain and wild
  rice
50 g (2 oz) basmati rice
large packet of fresh baby spinach
salt and freshly ground black pepper
20 g (¾ oz) butter

COOK'S TIP

Make sure you use cling film which is suitable for cooking purposes.

---

1 Bring 300 ml (½ pint) mixed fish stock and water to the boil in a saucepan. Add the mixed long grain and wild rice, cover and cook for about 18 minutes or until the liquid has been absorbed.

2 Bring the remaining fish stock and water to the boil, add the basmati rice, cover and cook for 9 minutes or until the liquid has been absorbed.

3 Meanwhile, bring a large pan of salted water to the boil. Add the spinach, cover and blanch for 1 minute. Drain well, then refresh under cold running water. Drain thoroughly, then transfer to a baking tray lined with a tea-towel to dry.

4 Line two 6 cm (2½ inch) metal rings (or biscuit cutters) with cling film. Carefully line the cling film with overlapping layers of spinach. Leave a good overhang to wrap over the top of the rice. (Set aside the leftover spinach to serve as an accompaniment.)

5 Mix all the cooked rice together while still warm. Toss in the butter and season well. Pack into the spinach-lined cutters and fold over the spinach leaves.

6 Fold over the cling film, place in a steamer basket and steam for 5 minutes. Carefully turn out onto warmed serving plates and remove the cling film.

ASPARAGUS

50 g (2 oz) fine asparagus tips
salt

1 Bring a pan of salted water to the boil. Add the asparagus and cook for 3 minutes.

2 Drain the asparagus, refresh under cold running water, then drain thoroughly. Toss in the dish in which the salmon was cooked to heat through before serving.

PASSION FRUIT AND CITRUS PUDDINGS

60 g (2½ oz) butter
60 g (2½ oz) light muscovado sugar
grated rind of 1 orange and 1 lime
3 passion fruit
2 drops of orange flower water
2 eggs (size 2)
60 g (2½ oz) ground almonds
1.25 ml (¼ tsp) ground cinnamon

Cointreau Sauce:
4 egg yolks
20 g (¾ oz) caster sugar
300 ml (½ pint) milk
30 ml (2 tbsp) Cointreau or other
   orange-flavoured liqueur
30 ml (2 tbsp) whipped cream

1 Butter 2 ramekins well and line with a disc of non-stick baking parchment.

2 Place the butter and sugar in a bowl and beat together until fluffy. Beat in the grated rinds.

3 Cut the passion fruit in half, scoop out the pulp and seeds and rub through a sieve. Add to the sugar mixture with the orange flower water and beat again. Whisk in the eggs and ground almonds a little at a time, then add the cinnamon.

4 Divide the mixture between the ramekins and cook in a preheated oven at 190°C (375°F) mark 5 for 20 minutes, or until the middle is still soft and moist but not runny.

5 Meanwhile prepare the sauce. Put the egg yolks and sugar in a bowl and beat together thoroughly until pale.

6 Place the milk in a heavy-based pan and bring to the boil. Remove from the heat and pour a little at a time on to the egg and sugar, whisking all the time. Return to the pan and heat gently, stirring, until the sauce thickens slightly and thinly coats the back of the spoon. Strain if necessary and stir to prevent curdling. Add the Cointreau and whipped cream. If not serving immediately, pour into a cold jug and cover to prevent a skin from forming.

7 Leave the puddings for a few minutes to cool slightly, then turn out onto warmed serving plates and surround with the Cointreau sauce.

The Final

Contestants

Jenna Tinson • Jessica Davies • Ross Spence

Panel of Judges

Michel Roux Jnr • Terence Conran • Loyd Grossman

Jessica Davies' Menu

MAIN COURSE

Lemon Sole with Creamy Dill and Grape Sauce

Medley of Vegetables

"The lemon sole was lovely" **Michel Roux Jnr**

DESSERT

Apricot Upside-down Pudding with Hot Syrup Sauce

"That was excellent and it looked terrific" **Terence Conran**

LEMON SOLE WITH CREAMY DILL AND GRAPE SAUCE

2 large sole fillets
25 g (1 oz) butter
10 ml (2 tsp) finely chopped dill
25 g (1 oz) plain flour
125 ml (4 fl oz) dry white wine
salt and freshly ground black pepper
250 ml (8 fl oz) milk
50 g (2 oz) seedless white grapes

To Garnish:
2 lemon slices
few grapes
2 dill sprigs

1 Place the fish in a greased oven-proof dish, cover and cook in a preheated oven at 180°C (350°F) mark 4 for 15-20 minutes.

2 Melt the butter in a saucepan, add the dill and cook for 1 minute. Add the flour and mix to form a smooth paste. Gradually stir in the wine and season with salt and pepper to taste. Add the milk and bring to the boil, stirring all the time. Cook, stirring, until smooth and thickened.

3 Add the grapes to the sauce just before serving and spoon over the cooked fish. Serve garnished with lemon, grapes and dill. Accompany with a medley of vegetables.

APRICOT UPSIDE-DOWN PUDDING WITH HOT SYRUP SAUCE

90 ml (3 fl oz) golden syrup
  (approximately)
6 canned apricot halves
50 g (2 oz) self-raising flour
50 g (2 oz) caster sugar
50 g (2 oz) margarine
1 egg (size 1)
juice of 1 lemon

1 Thoroughly grease 2 small ramekin dishes. Place a heaped tablespoonful of golden syrup in each dish and add the apricot halves.

2 Place the flour, sugar, margarine and egg in a bowl and beat well until light and fluffy. Spread evenly over the syrup and apricots.

3 Bake in a preheated oven at 180°C (350°F) mark 4 for 15 minutes or until the sponge has risen and is golden.

4 Meanwhile make the sauce. Put 3 heaped tablespoonfuls of golden syrup in a saucepan with the lemon juice. Heat gently until evenly blended.

5 Invert the puddings onto 2 warmed serving plates and serve immediately, with the hot syrup sauce.

The Final

Contestants
Jenna Tinson • Jessica Davies • Ross Spence

Panel of Judges
Michel Roux Jnr • Terence Conran • Loyd Grossman

Ross Spence's Menu

MAIN COURSE
Steamed Halibut with a Tarragon Mousse and a Wild Mushroom
Sauce, served with Vegetable Julienne

"The mushroom sauce was very good" **Michel Roux Jnr**

DESSERT
Rhubarb and Ginger Purse with an Orange and Coriander Sauce

"It was an egg custard sauce cooked to perfection" **Michel Roux Jnr**

STEAMED HALIBUT WITH A TARRAGON MOUSSE

2 halibut fillets, each 175 g (6 oz)

Tarragon Mousse:
125 g (4 oz) filleted halibut (trimmings)
1 egg white
1 tarragon sprig
50 ml (2 fl oz) double cream
salt and freshly ground black pepper

Sauce:
65 g (2½ oz) butter
2 shallots, chopped
175 g (6 oz) wild mushrooms
50 ml (2 fl oz) white wine
300 ml (½ pint) fish stock
150 ml (¼ pint) double cream

Vegetable Medley:
1 carrot, cut into julienne
½ leek, shredded
½ celeriac, shredded
25 g (1 oz) butter

To Garnish:
parsley sprig

1 To prepare the mousse, put the halibut trimmings, egg white and tarragon in a food processor and work until smooth. Transfer to a bowl and gradually fold in the cream. Season with salt and pepper to taste. Spread over the halibut fillets, using a warm palette knife. Place in a steamer and steam for about 10 minutes.

2 Meanwhile prepare the vegetable medley. Blanch the vegetables together in boiling water for about 3 minutes. Drain well. Melt the butter in a pan, add the vegetables, add salt and pepper to taste and sauté for about 2 minutes.

3 To prepare the sauce, melt 15 g (½ oz) of the butter in a pan, add the shallots and mushrooms, cover and sweat for 2 minutes. Add the wine and cook, uncovered, until reduced by half. Add the fish stock and reduce again by half. Add the cream and bring to the boil, then lower the heat and whisk in the remaining diced butter, a piece at a time.

4 To serve, pour the sauce onto a warmed serving dish, lay the fish on top and garnish with parsley. Arrange the vegetables on either side of the fish.

RHUBARB AND GINGER PURSE WITH AN ORANGE AND CORIANDER SAUCE

350 g (12 oz) rhubarb, trimmed and chopped
50 g (2 oz) caster sugar
4 pieces of preserved stem ginger in syrup, drained and diced
1 apple, peeled, cored and diced
4 sheets of filo pastry
melted butter, for brushing
icing sugar, for dusting

Orange and Coriander Sauce:
150 ml (¼ pint) milk
150 ml (¼ pint) double cream
3 egg yolks
75 g (3 oz) caster sugar
grated rind and juice of 1 orange
chopped coriander, to taste

To Decorate:
6 orange segments
coriander sprigs

1 Place the rhubarb, sugar and ginger in a pan and cook for about 15 minutes, until soft. Stir in the apple.

2 Brush one sheet of filo pastry with melted butter and dust with icing sugar. Lay another sheet on top then lay this inside an egg poaching ring. Spoon half of the filling into the centre. Bring the edges of the filo pastry up over the filling and twist together at the top to form a purse. Dust with icing sugar. Repeat with the remaining pastry and filling.

3 Cook in a preheated oven at 400°C (200°F) mark 6 for 10-15 minutes, until crisp and golden.

4 To make the sauce, place the milk and cream in a pan and bring to the boil. Whisk the egg yolks and sugar together in a bowl. Gradually add the hot milk mixture, stirring well. Return to the pan and cook, stirring, until thickened enough to lightly coat the back of the spoon; do not allow to boil. Pass through a fine sieve into a bowl.

5 Place the orange juice in a small pan, bring to the boil, and boil until reduced by half. Stir into the sauce, with the orange rind. Leave to cool, then stir in the chopped coriander to taste.

6 To serve, pour the sauce onto 2 serving plates. Arrange the filo purses on top and decorate with orange segments and coriander sprigs to serve.

INDEX

OF RECIPE TITLES AND CONTESTANTS